The Pigeon by John Galsworthy

A Fantasy in Three Acts

John Galsworthy was born at Kingston Upon Thames in Surrey, England, on August 14th 1867 to a wealthy and well established family. His schooling was at Harrow and New College, Oxford before training as a barrister and being called to the bar in 1890. However, Law was not attractive to him and he travelled abroad becoming great friends with the novelist Joseph Conrad, then a first mate on a sailing ship.

In 1895 Galsworthy began an affair with Ada Nemesis Pearson Cooper, the wife of his cousin Major Arthur Galsworthy. The affair was kept a secret for 10 years till she at last divorced and they married on 23rd September 1905.

Galsworthy first published in 1897 with a collection of short stories entitled "The Four Winds". For the next 7 years he published these and all works under his pen name John Sinjohn. It was only upon the death of his father and the publication of "The Island Pharisees" in 1904 that he published as John Galsworthy.

His first play, The Silver Box in 1906 was a success and was followed by "The Man of Property" later that same year and was the first in the Forsyte trilogy. Whilst today he is far more well know as a Nobel Prize winning novelist then he was considered a playwright dealing with social issues and the class system. Here we publish Villa Rubein, a very fine story that captures Galsworthy's unique narrative and take on life of the time.

He is now far better known for his novels, particularly The Forsyte Saga, his trilogy about the eponymous family of the same name. These books, as with many of his other works, deal with social class, upper-middle class lives in particular. Although always sympathetic to his characters, he reveals their insular, snobbish, and somewhat greedy attitudes and suffocating moral codes. He is now viewed as one of the first from the Edwardian era to challenge some of the ideals of society depicted in the literature of Victorian England.

In his writings he campaigns for a variety of causes, including prison reform, women's rights, animal welfare, and the opposition of censorship as well as a recurring theme of an unhappy marriage from the women's side. During World War I he worked in a hospital in France as an orderly after being passed over for military service.

He was appointed to the Order of Merit in 1929, after earlier turning down a knighthood, and awarded the Nobel Prize in 1932 though he was too ill to attend.

John Galsworthy died from a brain tumour at his London home, Grove Lodge, Hampstead on January 31st 1933. In accordance with his will he was cremated at Woking with his ashes then being scattered over the South Downs from an aeroplane.

Index of Contents

Persons of the Play
Scene
Act I - Christmas Eve.
Act II - New Year's Day.
Act III - The First of April.
John Galsworthy – A Short Biography
John Galsworthy – A Concise Bibliography

PERSONS OF THE PLAY

CHRISTOPHER WELLWYN, an artist
ANN, his daughter
GUINEVERE MEGAN, a flower-seller
RORY MEGAN, her husband
FERRAND, an alien
TIMSON, once a cabman
EDWARD BERTLEY, a Canon
ALFRED CALWAY, a Professor
SIR THOMAS HOXTON, a Justice of the Peace
Also a police constable, three humble-men, and some curious persons

SCENE

The action passes in Wellwyn's Studio, and the street outside.

ACT I

It is the night of Christmas Eve, the SCENE is a Studio, flush with the street, having a skylight darkened by a fall of snow. There is no one in the room, the walls of which are whitewashed, above a floor of bare dark boards. A fire is cheerfully burning. On a model's platform stands an easel and canvas. There are busts and pictures; a screen, a little stool, two arm. chairs, and a long old-fashioned settle under the window. A door in one wall leads to the house, a door in the opposite wall to the model's dressing-room, and the street door is in the centre of the wall between. On a low table a Russian samovar is hissing, and beside it on a tray stands a teapot, with glasses, lemon, sugar, and a decanter of rum. Through a huge uncurtained window close to the street door the snowy lamplit street can be seen, and beyond it the river and a night of stars.

The sound of a latchkey turned in the lock of the street door, and **ANN WELLWYN** enters, a girl of seventeen, with hair tied in a ribbon and covered by a scarf. Leaving the door open, she turns up the electric light and goes to the fire. She throws of her scarf and long red cloak. She is dressed in a high evening frock of some soft white material. Her movements are quick and substantial. Her face, full of no nonsense, is decided and sincere, with deep-set eyes, and a capable, well-shaped forehead. Shredding of her gloves she warms her hands.

In the doorway appear the figures of two men. The first is rather short and slight, with a soft short beard, bright eyes, and a crumply face. Under his squash hat his hair is rather plentiful and rather grey. He wears an old brown ulster and woollen gloves, and is puffing at a hand-made cigarette. He is **ANN'S** father, **WELLWYN**, the artist. His companion is a well-wrapped clergyman of medium height and stoutish build, with a pleasant, rosy face, rather shining eyes, and rather chubby clean-shaped lips; in appearance, indeed, a grown-up boy. He is the Vicar of the parish—**CANON BERTLEY**.

BERTLEY
My dear Wellwyn, the whole question of reform is full of difficulty. When you have two men like Professor Calway and Sir Thomas Hoxton taking diametrically opposite points of view, as we've seen to-night, I confess, I—

WELLWYN
Come in, Vicar, and have some grog.

BERTLEY
Not to-night, thanks! Christmas tomorrow! Great temptation, though, this room! Goodnight, Wellwyn; good-night, Ann!

ANN
[Coming from the fire towards the tea-table.]
Good-night, Canon Bertley.

[He goes out, and **WELLWYN**, shutting the door after him, approaches the fire.

ANN [Sitting on the little stool, with her back to the fire, and making tea]
Daddy!

WELLWYN
My dear?

ANN
You say you liked Professor Calway's lecture. Is it going to do you any good, that's the question?

WELLWYN
I—I hope so, Ann.

ANN
I took you on purpose. Your charity's getting simply awful. Those two this morning cleared out all my housekeeping money.

WELLWYN
Um! Um! I quite understand your feeling.

ANN

They both had your card, so I couldn't refuse—didn't know what you'd said to them. Why don't you make it a rule never to give your card to anyone except really decent people, and—picture dealers, of course.

WELLWYN
My dear, I have—often.

ANN
Then why don't you keep it? It's a frightful habit. You are naughty, Daddy. One of these days you'll get yourself into most fearful complications.

WELLWYN
My dear, when they—when they look at you?

ANN
You know the house wants all sorts of things. Why do you speak to them at all?

WELLWYN
I don't—they speak to me.

[He takes of his ulster and hangs it over the back of an arm-chair.

ANN
They see you coming. Anybody can see you coming, Daddy. That's why you ought to be so careful. I shall make you wear a hard hat. Those squashy hats of yours are hopelessly inefficient.

WELLWYN [Gazing at his hat.]
Calway wears one.

ANN
As if anyone would beg of Professor Calway.

WELLWYN
Well-perhaps not. You know, Ann, I admire that fellow. Wonderful power of-of-theory! How a man can be so absolutely tidy in his mind! It's most exciting.

ANN
Has any one begged of you to-day?

WELLWYN [Doubtfully]
No—no.

ANN [After a long, severe look]
Will you have rum in your tea?

WELLWYN [Crestfallen]
Yes, my dear—a good deal.

ANN [Pouring out the rum, and handing him the glass]
Well, who was it?

WELLWYN
He didn't beg of me. [Losing himself in recollection.] Interesting old creature, Ann—real type. Old cabman.

ANN
Where?

WELLWYN
Just on the Embankment.

ANN
Of course! Daddy, you know the Embankment ones are always rotters.

WELLWYN
Yes, my dear; but this wasn't.

ANN
Did you give him your card?

WELLWYN
I—I—don't

ANN
Did you, Daddy?

WELLWYN
I'm rather afraid I may have!

ANN
May have! It's simply immoral.

WELLWYN
Well, the old fellow was so awfully human, Ann. Besides, I didn't give him any money—hadn't got any.

ANN
Look here, Daddy! Did you ever ask anybody for anything? You know you never did, you'd starve first. So would anybody decent. Then, why won't you see that people who beg are rotters?

WELLWYN
But, my dear, we're not all the same. They wouldn't do it if it wasn't natural to them. One likes to be friendly. What's the use of being alive if one isn't?

ANN
Daddy, you're hopeless.

WELLWYN
But, look here, Ann, the whole thing's so jolly complicated. According to Calway, we're to give the State all we can spare, to make the undeserving deserving. He's a Professor; he ought to know. But old Hoxton's always dinning it into me that we ought to support private organisations for helping the deserving, and damn the undeserving. Well, that's just the opposite. And he's a J.P. Tremendous experience. And the Vicar seems to be for a little bit of both. Well, what the devil—? My trouble is, whichever I'm with, he always converts me. [Ruefully.] And there's no fun in any of them.

ANN [Rising]
Oh! Daddy, you are so—don't you know that you're the despair of all social reformers?

[She envelops him.]

There's a tear in the left knee of your trousers. You're not to wear them again.

WELLWYN
Am I likely to?

ANN
I shouldn't be a bit surprised if it isn't your only pair. D'you know what I live in terror of?

[**WELLWYN** gives her a queer and apprehensive look.

ANN
That you'll take them off some day, and give them away in the street. Have you got any money?

[She feels in his coat, and he his trousers—they find nothing.

Do you know that your pockets are one enormous hole?

WELLWYN
No!

ANN
Spiritually.

WELLWYN
Oh! Ah! H'm!

ANN [Severely]
Now, look here, Daddy! [She takes him by his lapels.] Don't imagine that it isn't the most disgusting luxury on your part to go on giving away things as you do! You know what you really are, I suppose—a sickly sentimentalist!

WELLWYN [Breaking away from her, disturbed]
It isn't sentiment. It's simply that they seem to me so—so—jolly. If I'm to give up feeling sort of—nice in here [he touches his chest] about people—it doesn't matter who they are—then I don't know what I'm to do. I shall have to sit with my head in a bag.

ANN

I think you ought to.

WELLWYN

I suppose they see I like them—then they tell me things. After that, of course you can't help doing what you can.

ANN

Well, if you will love them up!

WELLWYN

My dear, I don't want to. It isn't them especially—why, I feel it even with old Calway sometimes. It's only Providence that he doesn't want anything of me—except to make me like himself—confound him!

ANN [Moving towards the door into the house—impressively]

What you don't see is that other people aren't a bit like you.

WELLWYN

Well, thank God!

ANN

It's so old-fashioned too! I'm going to bed—I just leave you to your conscience.

WELLWYN

Oh!

ANN

[Opening the door-severely.] Good-night—[with a certain weakening] you old—Daddy!

[She jumps at him, gives him a hug, and goes out.

[**WELLWYN** stands perfectly still. He first gazes up at the skylight, then down at the floor. Slowly he begins to shake his head, and mutter, as he moves towards the fire.

WELLWYN

Bad lot.... Low type—no backbone, no stability!

[There comes a fluttering knock on the outer door. As the sound slowly enters his consciousness, he begins to wince, as though he knew, but would not admit its significance. Then he sits down, covering his ears. The knocking does not cease. **WELLWYN** drops first one, then both hands, rises, and begins to sidle towards the door. The knocking becomes louder.

WELLWYN

Ah dear! Tt! Tt! Tt!

[After a look in the direction of **ANN's** disappearance, he opens the street door a very little way. By the light of the lamp there can be seen a young girl in dark clothes, huddled in a shawl to which the snow is clinging. She has on her arm a basket covered with a bit of sacking.

WELLWYN
I can't, you know; it's impossible.

[The **GIRL** says nothing, but looks at him with dark eyes.

WELLWYN [Wincing]
Let's see—I don't know you—do I?

[The **GIRL**, speaking in a soft, hoarse voice, with a faint accent of reproach: "Mrs. Megan—you give me this—" She holds out a dirty visiting card.

WELLWYN [Recoiling from the card]
Oh! Did I? Ah! When?

MRS MEGAN
You 'ad some vi'lets off of me larst spring. You give me 'arf a crown.

[A smile tries to visit her face.]

WELLWYN [Looking stealthily round]
Ah! Well, come in—just for a minute—it's very cold—and tell us what it is.

[She comes in stolidly, a Sphinx-like figure, with her pretty tragic little face.

WELLWYN
I don't remember you. [Looking closer.] Yes, I do. Only— you weren't the same-were you?

MRS MEGAN [Dully]
I seen trouble since.

WELLWYN
Trouble! Have some tea?

[He looks anxiously at the door into the house, then goes quickly to the table, and pours out a glass of tea, putting rum into it.

WELLWYN
[Handing her the tea.] Keeps the cold out! Drink it off!

[**MRS MEGAN** drinks it of, chokes a little, and almost immediately seems to get a size larger. **WELLWYN** watches her with his head held on one side, and a smile broadening on his face.

WELLWYN
Cure for all evils, um?

MRS MEGAN
It warms you.

[She smiles.

WELLWYN [Smiling back, and catching himself out]
Well! You know, I oughtn't.

MRS MEGAN [Conscious of the disruption of his personality, and withdrawing into her tragic abyss]
I wouldn't 'a come, but you told me if I wanted an 'and—

WELLWYN [Gradually losing himself in his own nature]
Let me see—corner of Flight Street, wasn't it?

MRS MEGAN [With faint eagerness]
Yes, sir, an' I told you about me vi'lets—it was a luvly spring-day.

WELLWYN
Beautiful! Beautiful! Birds singing, and the trees, &c.! We had quite a talk. You had a baby with you.

MRS MEGAN
Yes. I got married since then.

WELLWYN
Oh! Ah! Yes! [Cheerfully.] And how's the baby?

MRS MEGAN [Turning to stone]
I lost her.

WELLWYN
Oh! poor—Um!

MRS MEGAN [Impassive]
You said something abaht makin' a picture of me. [With faint eagerness.] So I thought I might come, in case you'd forgotten.

WELLWYN [Looking at, her intently]
Things going badly?

MRS MEGAN [Stripping the sacking off her basket]
I keep 'em covered up, but the cold gets to 'em. Thruppence—that's all I've took.

WELLWYN
Ho! Tt! Tt!

[He looks into the basket.

Christmas, too!

MRS MEGAN
They're dead.

WELLWYN [Drawing in his breath]
Got a good husband?

MRS MEGAN
He plays cards.

WELLWYN
Oh, Lord! And what are you doing out—with a cold like that?

[He taps his chest.]

MRS MEGAN
We was sold up this morning—he's gone off with 'is mates. Haven't took enough yet for a night's lodgin'.

WELLWYN [Correcting a spasmodic dive into his pockets]
But who buys flowers at this time of night?

[**MRS MEGAN** looks at him, and faintly smiles.]

WELLWYN [Rumpling his hair]
Saints above us! Here! Come to the fire!

[She follows him to the fire. He shuts the street door.

WELLWYN
Are your feet wet? [She nods.] Well, sit down here, and take them off. That's right.

[She sits on the stool. And after a slow look up at him, which has in it a deeper knowledge than belongs of right to her years, begins taking off her shoes and stockings. **WELLWYN** goes to the door into the house, opens it, and listens with a sort of stealthy casualness. He returns whistling, but not out loud. The **GIRL** has finished taking off her stockings, and turned her bare toes to the flames. She shuffles them back under her skirt.

WELLWYN
How old are you, my child?

MRS MEGAN
Nineteen, come Candlemas.

WELLWYN
And what's your name?

MRS MEGAN
Guinevere.

WELLWYN
What? Welsh?

MRS MEGAN
Yes—from Battersea.

WELLWYN
And your husband?

MRS MEGAN
No. Irish, 'e is. Notting Dale, 'e comes from.

WELLWYN
Roman Catholic?

MRS MEGAN
Yes. My 'usband's an atheist as well.

WELLWYN
I see. [Abstractedly.] How jolly! And how old is he—this young man of yours?

MRS MEGAN
'E'll be twenty soon.

WELLWYN
Babes in the wood! Does he treat you badly?

MRS MEGAN
No.

WELLWYN
Nor drink?

MRS MEGAN
No. He's not a bad one. Only he gets playin' cards then 'e'll fly the kite.

WELLWYN
I see. And when he's not flying it, what does he do?

MRS MEGAN [Touching her basket]
Same as me. Other jobs tires 'im.

WELLWYN
That's very nice!

[He checks himself.

Well, what am I to do with you?

MRS MEGAN
Of course, I could get me night's lodging if I like to do—the same as some of them.

WELLWYN
No! no! Never, my child! Never!

MRS MEGAN
It's easy that way.

WELLWYN
Heavens! But your husband! Um?

MRS MEGAN [With stoical vindictiveness]
He's after one I know of.

WELLWYN
Tt! What a pickle!

MRS MEGAN
I'll 'ave to walk about the streets.

WELLWYN [To himself]
Now how can I?

[**MRS MEGAN** looks up and smiles at him, as if she had already discovered that he is peculiar.

WELLWYN
You see, the fact is, I mustn't give you anything—because —well, for one thing I haven't got it. There are other reasons, but that's the—real one. But, now, there's a little room where my models dress. I wonder if you could sleep there. Come, and see.

[The **GIRL** gets up lingeringly, loth to leave the warmth. She takes up her wet stockings.

MRS MEGAN
Shall I put them on again?

WELLWYN
No, no; there's a nice warm pair of slippers. [Seeing the steam rising from her.] Why, you're wet all over. Here, wait a little!

[He crosses to the door into the house, and after stealthy listening, steps through. The **GIRL**, like a cat, steals back to the warmth of the fire. **WELLWYN** returns with a candle, a canary-coloured bath gown, and two blankets.

WELLWYN
Now then!

[He precedes her towards the door of the model's room.

Hsssh!

[He opens the door and holds up the candle to show her the room.

Will it do? There's a couch. You'll find some washing things. Make yourself quite at home. See!

[The **GIRL**, perfectly dumb, passes through with her basket—and her shoes and stockings. **WELLWYN** hands her the candle, blankets, and bath gown.

WELLWYN
Have a good sleep, child! Forget that you're alive!

[He closes the door, mournfully.

Done it again!

[He goes to the table, cuts a large slice of cake, knocks on the door, and hands it in.

Chow-chow!

[Then, as he walks away, he sights the opposite door.

Well—damn it, what could I have done? Not a farthing on me!

[He goes to the street door to shut it, but first opens it wide to confirm himself in his hospitality.

Night like this!

[A sputter of snow is blown in his face. A voice says: "Monsieur, pardon!" **WELLWYN** recoils spasmodically. A **FIGURE** moves from the lamp-post to the doorway. He is seen to be young and to have ragged clothes. He speaks again: "You do not remember me, Monsieur? My name is Ferrand—it was in Paris, in the Champs-Elysees—by the fountain.... When you came to the door, Monsieur—I am not made of iron.... Tenez, here is your card I have never lost it." He holds out to **WELLWYN** an old and dirty wing card. As inch by inch he has advanced into the doorway, the light from within falls on him, a tall gaunt young pagan with fair hair and reddish golden stubble of beard, a long ironical nose a little to one side, and large, grey, rather prominent eyes. There is a certain grace in his figure and movements; his clothes are nearly dropping off him.

WELLWYN [Yielding to a pleasant memory]
Ah! yes. By the fountain. I was sitting there, and you came and ate a roll, and drank the water.

FERRAND [With faint eagerness.]

My breakfast. I was in poverty— veree bad off. You gave me ten francs. I thought I had a little the right—

[WELLWYN makes a movement of disconcertion

—seeing you said that if I came to England—

WELLWYN
Um! And so you've come?

FERRAND
It was time that I consolidated my fortunes, Monsieur.

WELLWYN
And you—have—

[He stops embarrassed.

FERRAND [Shrugging his ragged shoulders]
One is not yet Rothschild.

WELLWYN [Sympathetically]
No. [Yielding to memory.] We talked philosophy.

FERRAND
I have not yet changed my opinion. We other vagabonds, we are exploited by the bourgeois. This is always my idea, Monsieur.

WELLWYN
Yes—not quite the general view, perhaps! Well— [Heartily.] Come in! Very glad to see you again.

FERRAND [Brushing his arms over his eyes]
Pardon, Monsieur—your goodness—I am a little weak.

[He opens his coat, and shows a belt drawn very tight over his ragged shirt.

I tighten him one hole for each meal, during two days now. That gives you courage.

WELLWYN [With cooing sounds, pouring out tea, and adding rum]
Have some of this. It'll buck you up.

[He watches the young man drink.

FERRAND [Becoming a size larger]
Sometimes I think that I will never succeed to dominate my life, Monsieur—though I have no vices, except that I guard always the aspiration to achieve success. But I will not roll myself under the machine of existence to gain a nothing every day. I must find with what to fly a little.

WELLWYN [Delicately]
Yes; yes—I remember, you found it difficult to stay long in any particular—yes.

FERRAND [Proudly]
In one little corner? No—Monsieur—never! That is not in my character. I must see life.

WELLWYN
Quite, quite! Have some cake?

[He cuts cake.

FERRAND
In your country they say you cannot eat the cake and have it. But one must always try, Monsieur; one must never be content. [Refusing the cake.] 'Grand merci', but for the moment I have no stomach—I have lost my stomach now for two days. If I could smoke, Monsieur!

[He makes the gesture of smoking.

WELLWYN
Rather!

[Handing his tobacco pouch.

Roll yourself one.

FERRAND [Rapidly rolling a cigarette.]
If I had not found you, Monsieur—I would have been a little hole in the river to-night— I was so discouraged.

[He inhales and puffs a long luxurious whif of smoke. Very bitterly.

Life!

[He disperses the puff of smoke with his finger, and stares before him.

And to think that in a few minutes HE will be born! Monsieur!

[He gazes intently at **WELLWYN**.

The world would reproach you for your goodness to me.

WELLWYN [Looking uneasily at the door into the house]
You think so? Ah!

FERRAND
Monsieur, if HE himself were on earth now, there would be a little heap of gentlemen writing to the journals every day to call Him sloppee sentimentalist! And what is veree funny, these gentlemen they would all be most strong Christians.

[He regards **WELLWYN** deeply.

But that will not trouble you, Monsieur; I saw well from the first that you are no Christian. You have so kind a face.

WELLWYN
Oh! Indeed!

FERRAND
You have not enough the Pharisee in your character. You do not judge, and you are judged.

[He stretches his limbs as if in pain.

WELLWYN
Are you in pain?

FERRAND
I 'ave a little the rheumatism.

WELLWYN
Wet through, of course!

[Glancing towards the house.

Wait a bit! I wonder if you'd like these trousers; they've—er—they're not quite—

[He passes through the door into the house. **FERRAND** stands at the fire, with his limbs spread as it were to embrace it, smoking with abandonment. **WELLWYN** returns stealthily, dressed in a Jaeger dressing-gown, and bearing a pair of drawers, his trousers, a pair of slippers, and a sweater.

WELLWYN [Speaking in a low voice, for the door is still open]
Can you make these do for the moment?

FERRAND
'Je vous remercie', Monsieur.

[Pointing to the screen.

May I retire?

WELLWYN
Yes, yes.

[**FERRAND** goes behind the screen. **WELLWYN** closes the door into the house, then goes to the window to draw the curtains. He suddenly recoils and stands petrified with doubt.

WELLWYN

Good Lord!

[There is the sound of tapping on glass. Against the window-pane is pressed the face of a man. **WELLWYN** motions to him to go away. He does not go, but continues tapping. **WELLWYN** opens the door. There enters a square old **MAN**, with a red, pendulous jawed, shaking face under a snow besprinkled bowler hat. He is holding out a visiting card with tremulous hand.

WELLWYN
Who's that? Who are you?

TIMSON [In a thick, hoarse, shaking voice]
'Appy to see you, sir; we 'ad a talk this morning. Timson—I give you me name. You invited of me, if ye remember.

WELLWYN
It's a little late, really.

TIMSON
Well, ye see, I never expected to 'ave to call on yer. I was 'itched up all right when I spoke to yer this mornin', but bein' Christmas, things 'ave took a turn with me to-day. [He speaks with increasing thickness.] I'm reg'lar disgusted—not got the price of a bed abaht me. Thought you wouldn't like me to be delicate—not at my age.

WELLWYN [With a mechanical and distracted dive of his hands into his pockets]
The fact is, it so happens I haven't a copper on me.

TIMSON [Evidently taking this for professional refusal]
Wouldn't arsk you if I could 'elp it. 'Ad to do with 'orses all me life. It's this 'ere cold I'm frightened of. I'm afraid I'll go to sleep.

WELLWYN
Well, really, I—

TIMSON
To be froze to death—I mean—it's awkward.

WELLWYN [Puzzled and unhappy]
Well—come in a moment, and let's— think it out. Have some tea!

[He pours out the remains of the tea, and finding there is not very much, adds rum rather liberally. **TIMSON**, who walks a little wide at the knees, steadying his gait, has followed.

TIMSON [Receiving the drink]
Yer 'ealth. 'Ere's—soberiety!

[He applies the drink to his lips with shaking hand. Agreeably surprised.

Blimey! Thish yer tea's foreign, ain't it?

FERRAND [Reappearing from behind the screen in his new clothes of which the trousers stop too soon]
With a needle, Monsieur, I would soon have with what to make face against the world.

WELLWYN
Too short! Ah!

[He goes to the dais on which stands Ann's workbasket, and takes from it a needle and cotton.

[While he is so engaged **FERRAND** is sizing up old **TIMSON**, as one dog will another. The old man, glass in hand, seems to have lapsed into coma.

FERRAND [Indicating **TIMSON**]
Monsieur!

[He makes the gesture of one drinking, and shakes his head.

WELLWYN [Handing him the needle and cotton]
Um! Afraid so!

[They approach **TIMSON**, who takes no notice.

FERRAND [Gently]
It is an old cabby, is it not, Monsieur? 'Ceux sont tous des buveurs'.

WELLWYN [Concerned at the old man's stupefaction]
Now, my old friend, sit down a moment.

[They manoeuvre **TIMSON** to the settee]

Will you smoke?

TIMSON [In a drowsy voice]
Thank 'ee-smoke pipe of 'baccer. Old 'orse—standin' abaht in th' cold.

[He relapses into coma.

FERRAND [With a click of his tongue]
'Il est parti'.

WELLWYN [Doubtfully]
He hasn't really left a horse outside, do you think?

FERRAND
Non, non, Monsieur—no 'orse. He is dreaming. I know very well that state of him—that catches you sometimes. It is the warmth sudden on the stomach. He will speak no more sense to-night. At the most, drink, and fly a little in his past.

WELLWYN
Poor old buffer!

FERRAND
Touching, is it not, Monsieur? There are many brave gents among the old cabbies—they have philosophy—that comes from 'orses, and from sitting still.

WELLWYN [Touching **TIMSON's** shoulder]
Drenched!

FERRAND
That will do 'im no 'arm, Monsieur-no 'arm at all. He is well wet inside, remember—it is Christmas to-morrow. Put him a rug, if you will, he will soon steam.

[**WELLWYN** takes up **ANN's** long red cloak, and wraps it round the old **MAN.**

TIMSON [Faintly roused]
Tha's right. Put—the rug on th' old 'orse.

[He makes a strange noise, and works his head and tongue.

WELLWYN [Alarmed]
What's the matter with him?

FERRAND
It is nothing, Monsieur; for the moment he thinks 'imself a 'orse. 'Il joue "cache-cache,"' 'ide and seek, with what you call— 'is bitt.

WELLWYN
But what's to be done with him? One can't turn him out in this state.

FERRAND
If you wish to leave him 'ere, Monsieur, have no fear. I charge myself with him.

WELLWYN
Oh! [Dubiously.] You—er—I really don't know, I—hadn't contemplated—You think you could manage if I—if I went to bed?

FERRAND
But certainly, Monsieur.

WELLWYN [Still dubiously]
You—you're sure you've everything you want?

FERRAND [Bowing]
'Mais oui, Monsieur'.

WELLWYN

I don't know what I can do by staying.

FERRAND
There is nothing you can do, Monsieur. Have confidence in me.

WELLWYN
Well-keep the fire up quietly—very quietly. You'd better take this coat of mine, too. You'll find it precious cold, I expect, about three o'clock.

[He hands **FERRAND** his Ulster.

FERRAND [Taking it]
I shall sleep in praying for you, Monsieur.

WELLWYN
Ah! Yes! Thanks! Well-good-night! By the way, I shall be down rather early. Have to think of my household a bit, you know.

FERRAND
'Tres bien, Monsieur'. I comprehend. One must well be regular in this life.

WELLWYN [With a start]
Lord!

[He looks at the door of the model's room.

I'd forgotten—

FERRAND
Can I undertake anything, Monsieur?

WELLWYN
No, no!

[He goes to the electric light switch by the outer door.

You won't want this, will you?

FERRAND
'Merci, Monsieur'.

[**WELLWYN** switches off the light.

FERRAND
'Bon soir, Monsieur'!

WELLWYN
The devil! Er—good-night!

[He hesitates, rumples his hair, and passes rather suddenly away.

FERRAND [To himself] Poor pigeon!

[Looking long at old **TIMSON**

'Espece de type anglais!'

[He sits down in the firelight, curls up a foot on his knee, and taking out a knife, rips the stitching of a turned-up end of trouser, pinches the cloth double, and puts in the preliminary stitch of a new hem—all with the swiftness of one well-accustomed. Then, as if hearing a sound behind him, he gets up quickly and slips behind the screen. **MRS MEGAN**, attracted by the cessation of voices, has opened the door, and is creeping from the model's room towards the fire. She has almost reached it before she takes in the torpid crimson figure of old **TIMSON**. She halts and puts her hand to her chest—a queer figure in the firelight, garbed in the canary-coloured bath gown and rabbit's-wool slippers, her black matted hair straggling down on her neck. Having quite digested the fact that the old man is in a sort of stupor, **MRS MEGAN** goes close to the fire, and sits on the little stool, smiling sideways at old **TIMSON**. **FERRAND**, coming quietly up behind, examines her from above, drooping his long nose as if enquiring with it as to her condition in life; then he steps back a yard or two.

FERRAND [Gently]
'Pardon, Ma'moiselle'.

MRS MEGAN [Springing to her feet]
Oh!

FERRAND
All right, all right! We are brave gents!

TIMSON [Faintly roused]
'Old up, there!

FERRAND
Trust in me, Ma'moiselle!

[**MRS MEGAN** responds by drawing away.

FERRAND [Gently]
We must be good comrades. This asylum—it is better than a doss-'ouse.

[He pushes the stool over towards her, and seats himself. Somewhat reassured, **MRS MEGAN** again sits down.

MRS MEGAN
You frightened me.

TIMSON [Unexpectedly-in a drowsy tone]

Purple foreigners!

FERRAND
Pay no attention, Ma'moiselle. He is a philosopher.

MRS MEGAN
Oh! I thought 'e was boozed.

[They both look at **TIMSON**.

FERRAND
It is the same-veree 'armless.

MRS MEGAN
What's that he's got on 'im?

FERRAND
It is a coronation robe. Have no fear, Ma'moiselle. Veree docile potentate.

MRS MEGAN
I wouldn't be afraid of him.

[Challenging **FERRAND**.

I'm afraid o' you.

FERRAND
It is because you do not know me, Ma'moiselle. You are wrong, it is always the unknown you should love.

MRS MEGAN
I don't like the way you-speaks to me.

FERRAND
Ah! You are a Princess in disguise?

MRS MEGAN
No fear!

FERRAND
No? What is it then you do to make face against the necessities of life? A living?

MRS MEGAN
Sells flowers.

FERRAND [Rolling his eyes]
It is not a career.

MRS MEGAN [With a touch of devilry]
You don't know what I do.

FERRAND
Ma'moiselle, whatever you do is charming.

[**MRS MEGAN** looks at him, and slowly smiles.

MRS MEGAN
You're a foreigner.

FERRAND
It is true.

MRS MEGAN
What do you do for a livin'?

FERRAND
I am an interpreter.

MRS MEGAN
You ain't very busy, are you?

FERRAND [With dignity]
At present I am resting.

MRS MEGAN [Looking at him and smiling]
How did you and 'im come here?

FERRAND
Ma'moiselle, we would ask you the same question.

MRS MEGAN
The gentleman let me. 'E's funny.

FERRAND
'C'est un ange'

[At **MRS MEGAN's** blank stare he interprets.

An angel!

MRS MEGAN
Me luck's out-that's why I come.

FERRAND [Rising]
Ah! Ma'moiselle! Luck! There is the little God who dominates us all. Look at this old!

[He points to **TIMSON**]

He is finished. In his day that old would be doing good business. He could afford himself—

[He makes a sign of drinking.

—Then come the motor cars. All goes—he has nothing left, only 'is 'abits of a 'cocher'! Luck!

TIMSON [With a vague gesture—drowsily]
Kick the foreign beggars out.

FERRAND
A real Englishman.... And look at me! My father was merchant of ostrich feathers in Brussels. If I had been content to go in his business, I would 'ave been rich. But I was born to roll—"rolling stone" to voyage is stronger than myself. Luck!... And you, Ma'moiselle, shall I tell your fortune? [He looks in her face.] You were born for 'la joie de vivre'—to drink the wines of life. 'Et vous voila'! Luck!

[Though she does not in the least understand what he has said, her expression changes to a sort of glee.

FERRAND
Yes. You were born loving pleasure. Is it not? You see, you cannot say, No. All of us, we have our fates. Give me your hand. [He kneels down and takes her hand.] In each of us there is that against which we cannot struggle. Yes, yes!

[He holds her hand, and turns it over between his own. **MRS MEGAN** remains stolid, half fascinated, half-reluctant.

TIMSON [Flickering into consciousness]
Be'ave yourselves! Yer crimson canary birds!

[**MRS MEGAN** would withdraw her hand, but cannot.

FERRAND
Pay no attention, Ma'moiselle. He is a Puritan.

[**TIMSON** relapses into comatosity, upsetting his glass, which falls with a crash.

MRS MEGAN
Let go my hand, please!

FERRAND [Relinquishing it, and staring into the fore gravely]
There is one thing I have never done—'urt a woman—that is hardly in my character. [Then, drawing a little closer, he looks into her face.] Tell me, Ma'moiselle, what is it you think of all day long?

MRS MEGAN
I dunno—lots, I thinks of.

FERRAND

Shall I tell you?

[Her eyes remain fixed on his, the strangeness of him preventing her from telling him to "get along." He goes on in his ironic voice.] It is of the streets—the lights— the faces—it is of all which moves, and is warm—it is of colour—it is [he brings his face quite close to hers] of Love. That is for you what the road is for me. That is for you what the rum is for that old—[He jerks his thumb back at TIMSON Then bending swiftly forward to the GIRL.

See! I kiss you—Ah!

[He draws her forward off the stool. There is a little struggle, then she resigns her lips. The little stool, overturned, falls with a clatter. They spring up, and move apart. The door opens and ANN enters from the house in a blue dressing-gown, with her hair loose, and a candle held high above her head. Taking in the strange half-circle round the stove, she recoils. Then, standing her ground, calls in a voice sharpened by fright: "Daddy—Daddy!"

TIMSON [Stirring uneasily, and struggling to his feet]
All right! I'm comin'!

FERRAND
Have no fear, Madame!

[In the silence that follows, a clock begins loudly striking twelve. ANN remains, as if carved in atone, her eyes fastened on the strangers. There is the sound of someone falling downstairs, and WELLWYN appears, also holding a candle above his head.

ANN
Look!

WELLWYN
Yes, yes, my dear! It—it happened.

ANN [With a sort of groan]
Oh! Daddy!

[In the renewed silence, the church clock ceases to chime.

FERRAND [Softly, in his ironic voice]
HE is come, Monsieur! 'Appy Christmas! Bon Noel!

[There is a sudden chime of bells. The Stage is blotted dark.

Curtain.

ACT II

It is four o'clock in the afternoon of New Year's Day. On the raised dais **MRS MEGAN** is standing, in her rags; with bare feet and ankles, her dark hair as if blown about, her lips parted, holding out a dishevelled bunch of violets. Before his easel, **WELLWYN** is painting her. Behind him, at a table between the cupboard and the door to the model's room, **TIMSON** is washing brushes, with the movements of one employed upon relief works. The samovar is hissing on the table by the stove, the tea things are set out.

WELLWYN
Open your mouth.

[**MRS MEGAN** opens her mouth.

ANN [In hat and coat, entering from the house]
Daddy!

[**WELLWYN** goes to her; and, released from restraint, **MRS MEGAN** looks round at **TIMSON** and grimaces.

WELLWYN
Well, my dear?

[They speak in low voices.

ANN [Holding out a note]
This note from Canon Bentley. He's going to bring her husband here this afternoon.

[She looks at **MRS MEGAN**.

WELLWYN
Oh!

[He also looks at **MRS MEGAN**.

ANN
And I met Sir Thomas Hoxton at church this morning, and spoke to him about Timson.

WELLWYN
Um!

[They look at **TIMSON**. Then **ANN** goes back to the door, and **WELLWYN** follows her.

ANN [Turning]
I'm going round now, Daddy, to ask Professor Calway what we're to do with that Ferrand.

WELLWYN
Oh! One each! I wonder if they'll like it.

ANN
They'll have to lump it.

[She goes out into the house.

WELLWYN [Back at his easel]
You can shut your mouth now.

[**MRS MEGAN** shuts her mouth, but opens it immediately to smile]

WELLWYN [Spasmodically]
Ah! Now that's what I want.

[He dabs furiously at the canvas. Then standing back, runs his hands through his hair and turns a painter's glance towards the skylight.

Dash! Light's gone! Off you get, child—don't tempt me!

[**MRS MEGAN** descends. Passing towards the door of the model's room she stops, and stealthily looks at the picture.

TIMSON
Ah! Would yer!

WELLWYN [Wheeling round]
Want to have a look? Well—come on!

[He takes her by the arm, and they stand before the canvas. After a stolid moment, she giggles.

WELLWYN
Oh! You think so?

MRS MEGAN [Who has lost her hoarseness]
It's not like my picture that I had on the pier.

WELLWYN
No-it wouldn't be.

MRS MEGAN [Timidly]
If I had an 'at on, I'd look better.

WELLWYN
With feathers?

MRS MEGAN
Yes.

WELLWYN
Well, you can't! I don't like hats, and I don't like feathers.

[**MRS MEGAN** timidly tugs his sleeve. **TIMSON**, screened as he thinks by the picture, has drawn from his bulky pocket a bottle and is taking a stealthy swig.

WELLWYN [To **MRS MEGAN**, affecting not to notice]
How much do I owe you?

MRS MEGAN [A little surprised]
You paid me for to-day-all 'cept a penny.

WELLWYN
Well! Here it is.

[He gives her a coin]

Go and get your feet on!

MRS MEGAN
You've give me 'arf a crown.

WELLWYN
Cut away now!

[**MRS MEGAN**, smiling at the coin, goes towards the model's room. She looks back at **WELLWYN**, as if to draw his eyes to her, but he is gazing at the picture; then, catching old **TIMSON'S** sour glance, she grimaces at him, kicking up her feet with a little squeal. But when **WELLWYN** turns to the sound, she is demurely passing through the doorway.

TIMSON [In his voice of dubious sobriety]
I've finished these yer brushes, sir. It's not a man's work. I've been thinkin' if you'd keep an 'orse, I could give yer satisfaction.

WELLWYN
Would the horse, Timson?

TIMSON [Looking him up and down]
I knows of one that would just suit yer. Reel 'orse, you'd like 'im.

WELLWYN [Shaking his head]
Afraid not, Timson! Awfully sorry, though, to have nothing better for you than this, at present.

TIMSON [Faintly waving the brushes]
Of course, if you can't afford it, I don't press you—it's only that I feel I'm not doing meself justice. [Confidentially.] There's just one thing, sir; I can't bear to see a gen'leman imposed on. That foreigner—'e's not the sort to 'ave about the place. Talk? Oh! ah! But 'e'll never do any good with 'imself. He's a alien.

WELLWYN
Terrible misfortune to a fellow, Timson.

TIMSON

Don't you believe it, sir; it's his fault I says to the young lady yesterday: Miss Ann, your father's a gen'leman [with a sudden accent of hoarse sincerity], and so you are—I don't mind sayin' it—but, I said, he's too easy-goin'.

WELLWYN

Indeed!

TIMSON

Well, see that girl now! [He shakes his head.] I never did believe in goin' behind a person's back—I'm an Englishman—but [lowering his voice] she's a bad hat, sir. Why, look at the street she comes from!

WELLWYN

Oh! you know it.

TIMSON

Lived there meself larst three years. See the difference a few days' corn's made in her. She's that saucy you can't touch 'er head.

WELLWYN

Is there any necessity, Timson?

TIMSON

Artful too. Full o' vice, I call'er. Where's 'er 'usband?

WELLWYN [Gravely]

Come, Timson! You wouldn't like her to—

TIMSON [With dignity, so that the bottle in his pocket is plainly visible]

I'm a man as always beared inspection.

WELLWYN [With a well-directed smile]

So I see.

TIMSON [Curving himself round the bottle]

It's not for me to say nothing—but I can tell a gen'leman as quick as ever I can tell an 'orse.

WELLWYN [Painting]

I find it safest to assume that every man is a gentleman, and every woman a lady. Saves no end of self-contempt. Give me the little brush.

TIMSON [Handing him the brush—after a considerable introspective pause]

Would yer like me to stay and wash it for yer again? [With great resolution.] I will—I'll do it for you—never grudged workin' for a gen'leman.

WELLWYN [With sincerity]

Thank you, Timson—very good of you, I'm sure.

[He hands him back the brush.

Just lend us a hand with this.

[Assisted by **TIMSON** he pushes back the dais.

Let's see! What do I owe you?

TIMSON [Reluctantly]
It so 'appens, you advanced me to-day's yesterday.

WELLWYN
Then I suppose you want to-morrow's?

TIMSON
Well, I 'ad to spend it, lookin' for a permanent job. When you've got to do with 'orses, you can't neglect the publics, or you might as well be dead.

WELLWYN
Quite so!

TIMSON
It mounts up in the course o' the year.

WELLWYN
It would.

[Passing him a coin.

This is for an exceptional purpose—Timson—see. Not—

TIMSON [Touching his forehead]
Certainly, sir. I quite understand. I'm not that sort, as I think I've proved to yer, comin' here regular day after day, all the week. There's one thing, I ought to warn you perhaps—I might 'ave to give this job up any day.

[He makes a faint demonstration with the little brush, then puts it, absent-mindedly, into his pocket.

WELLWYN [Gravely]
I'd never stand in the way of your bettering yourself, Timson. And, by the way, my daughter spoke to a friend about you to-day. I think something may come of it.

TIMSON
Oh! Oh! She did! Well, it might do me a bit o' good. [He makes for the outer door, but stops.] That foreigner! 'E sticks in my gizzard. It's not as if there wasn't plenty o' pigeons for 'im to pluck in 'is own Gawd-forsaken country. Reg-lar jay, that's what I calls 'im. I could tell yer something—

[He has opened the door, and suddenly sees that **FERRAND** himself is standing there. Sticking out his lower lip, **TIMSON** gives a roll of his jaw and lurches forth into the street. Owing to a slight miscalculation, his face and raised arms are plainly visible through the window, as he fortifies himself from his battle against the cold. **FERRAND**, having closed the door, stands with his thumb acting as pointer towards this spectacle. He is now remarkably dressed in an artist's squashy green hat, a frock coat too small for him, a bright blue tie of knitted silk, the grey trousers that were torn, well-worn brown boots, and a tan waistcoat.

WELLWYN
What luck to-day?

FERRAND [With a shrug]
Again I have beaten all London, Monsieur —not one bite. [Contemplating himself.] I think perhaps, that, for the bourgeoisie, there is a little too much colour in my costume.

WELLWYN [Contemplating him]
Let's see—I believe I've an old top hat somewhere.

FERRAND
Ah! Monsieur, 'merci', but that I could not. It is scarcely in my character.

WELLWYN
True!

FERRAND
I have been to merchants of wine, of tabac, to hotels, to Leicester Square. I have been to a Society for spreading Christian knowledge—I thought there I would have a chance perhaps as interpreter. 'Toujours meme chose', we regret, we have no situation for you—same thing everywhere. It seems there is nothing doing in this town.

WELLWYN
I've noticed, there never is.

FERRAND
I was thinking, Monsieur, that in aviation there might be a career for me—but it seems one must be trained.

WELLWYN
Afraid so, Ferrand.

FERRAND [Approaching the picture]
Ah! You are always working at this. You will have something of very good there, Monsieur. You wish to fix the type of wild savage existing ever amongst our high civilisation. 'C'est tres chic ca'!

[**WELLWYN** manifests the quiet delight of an English artist actually understood.

In the figures of these good citizens, to whom she offers her flower, you would give the idea of all the cage doors open to catch and make tame the wild bird, that will surely die within. 'Tres gentil'! Believe me, Monsieur, you have there the greatest comedy of life! How anxious are the tame birds to do the wild birds good. [His voice changes.] For the wild birds it is not funny. There is in some human souls, Monsieur, what cannot be made tame.

WELLWYN
I believe you, Ferrand.

[The face of a young man appears at the window, unseen. Suddenly **ANN** opens the door leading to the house.

ANN
Daddy—I want you.

WELLWYN [To **FERRAND**]
Excuse me a minute!

[He goes to his daughter, and they pass out. **FERRAND** remains at the picture. **MRS MEGAN** dressed in some of Ann's discarded garments, has come out of the model's room. She steals up behind **FERRAND** like a cat, reaches an arm up, and curls it round his mouth. He turns, and tries to seize her; she disingenuously slips away. He follows. The chase circles the tea table. He catches her, lifts her up, swings round with her, so that her feet fly out; kisses her bent-back face, and sets her down. She stands there smiling. The face at the window darkens.

FERRAND
La Valse!

[He takes her with both hands by the waist, she puts her hands against his shoulders to push him of—and suddenly they are whirling. As they whirl, they bob together once or twice, and kiss. Then, with a warning motion towards the door, she wrenches herself free, and stops beside the picture, trying desperately to appear demure. **WELLWYN** and **ANN** have entered. The face has vanished.

FERRAND [Pointing to the picture]
One does not comprehend all this, Monsieur, without well studying. I was in train to interpret for Ma'moiselle the chiaroscuro.

WELLWYN [With a queer look]
Don't take it too seriously, Ferrand.

FERRAND
It is a masterpiece.

WELLWYN
My daughter's just spoken to a friend, Professor Calway. He'd like to meet you. Could you come back a little later?

FERRAND
Certainly, Ma'moiselle. That will be an opening for me, I trust.

[He goes to the street door.

ANN [Paying no attention to him]
Mrs. Megan, will you too come back in half an hour?

FERRAND
'Tres bien, Ma'moiselle'! I will see that she does. We will take a little promenade together. That will do us good.

[He motions towards the door; **MRS MEGAN**, all eyes, follows him out.

ANN
Oh! Daddy, they are rotters. Couldn't you see they were having the most high jinks?

WELLWYN [At his picture]
I seemed to have noticed something.

ANN [Preparing for tea]
They were kissing.

WELLWYN
Tt! Tt!

ANN
They're hopeless, all three—especially her. Wish I hadn't given her my clothes now.

WELLWYN [Absorbed]
Something of wild-savage.

ANN
Thank goodness it's the Vicar's business to see that married people live together in his parish.

WELLWYN
Oh! [Dubiously.] The Megans are Roman Catholic-Atheists, Ann.

ANN [With heat]
Then they're all the more bound.

[**WELLWYN** gives a sudden and alarmed whistle.

ANN
What's the matter?

WELLWYN
Didn't you say you spoke to Sir Thomas, too. Suppose he comes in while the Professor's here. They're cat and dog.

ANN [Blankly]

Oh!

[As **WELLWYN** strikes a match

The samovar is lighted

[Taking up the nearly empty decanter of rum and going to the cupboard.

It's all right. He won't.

WELLWYN
We'll hope not.

[He turns back to his picture.

ANN [At the cupboard]
Daddy!

WELLWYN
Hi!

ANN
There were three bottles.

WELLWYN
Oh!

ANN
Well! Now there aren't any.

WELLWYN [Abstracted]
That'll be Timson.

ANN [With real horror]
But it's awful!

WELLWYN
It is, my dear.

ANN
In seven days. To say nothing of the stealing.

WELLWYN [Vexed]
I blame myself-very much. Ought to have kept it locked up.

ANN
You ought to keep him locked up!

[He goes to the street door.

ANN [Paying no attention to him]
Mrs. Megan, will you too come back in half an hour?

FERRAND
'Tres bien, Ma'moiselle'! I will see that she does. We will take a little promenade together. That will do us good.

[He motions towards the door; **MRS MEGAN**, all eyes, follows him out.

ANN
Oh! Daddy, they are rotters. Couldn't you see they were having the most high jinks?

WELLWYN [At his picture]
I seemed to have noticed something.

ANN [Preparing for tea]
They were kissing.

WELLWYN
Tt! Tt!

ANN
They're hopeless, all three—especially her. Wish I hadn't given her my clothes now.

WELLWYN [Absorbed]
Something of wild-savage.

ANN
Thank goodness it's the Vicar's business to see that married people live together in his parish.

WELLWYN
Oh! [Dubiously.] The Megans are Roman Catholic-Atheists, Ann.

ANN [With heat]
Then they're all the more bound.

[**WELLWYN** gives a sudden and alarmed whistle.

ANN
What's the matter?

WELLWYN
Didn't you say you spoke to Sir Thomas, too. Suppose he comes in while the Professor's here. They're cat and dog.

ANN [Blankly]

Oh!

[As **WELLWYN** strikes a match

The samovar is lighted

[Taking up the nearly empty decanter of rum and going to the cupboard.

It's all right. He won't.

WELLWYN
We'll hope not.

[He turns back to his picture.

ANN [At the cupboard]
Daddy!

WELLWYN
Hi!

ANN
There were three bottles.

WELLWYN
Oh!

ANN
Well! Now there aren't any.

WELLWYN [Abstracted]
That'll be Timson.

ANN [With real horror]
But it's awful!

WELLWYN
It is, my dear.

ANN
In seven days. To say nothing of the stealing.

WELLWYN [Vexed]
I blame myself-very much. Ought to have kept it locked up.

ANN
You ought to keep him locked up!

[There is heard a mild but authoritative knock.

WELLWYN
Here's the Vicar!

ANN
What are you going to do about the rum?

WELLWYN [Opening the door to **CANON BERTLEY**]
Come in, Vicar! Happy New Year!

BERTLEY
Same to you! Ah! Ann! I've got into touch with her young husband—he's coming round.

ANN [Still a little out of her place]
Thank Go—Moses!

BERTLEY [Faintly surprised]
From what I hear he's not really a bad youth. Afraid he bets on horses. The great thing, Wellwyn, with those poor fellows is to put your finger on the weak spot.

ANN [To herself-gloomily]
That's not difficult. What would you do, Canon Bertley, with a man who's been drinking father's rum?

BERTLEY
Remove the temptation, of course.

WELLWYN
He's done that.

BERTLEY
Ah! Then—

[**WELLWYN** and **ANN** hang on his words.

—then I should—er—

ANN [Abruptly]
Remove him.

BERTLEY
Before I say that, Ann, I must certainly see the individual.

WELLWYN [Pointing to the window]
There he is!

[In the failing light **TIMSON'S** face is indeed to be seen pressed against the window pane.

ANN

Daddy, I do wish you'd have thick glass put in. It's so disgusting to be spied at!

[**WELLWYN** going quickly to the door, has opened it.

What do you want?

[**TIMSON** enters with dignity. He is fuddled.

TIMSON [Slowly]

Arskin' yer pardon-thought it me duty to come back-found thish yer little brishel on me.

[He produces the little paint brush.

ANN [In a deadly voice]

Nothing else?

[**TIMSON** accords her a glassy stare.

WELLWYN [Taking the brush hastily]

That'll do, Timson, thanks!

TIMSON

As I am 'ere, can I do anything for yer?

ANN

Yes, you can sweep out that little room. [She points to the model's room.] There's a broom in there.

TIMSON [Disagreeably surprised]

Certainly; never make bones about a little extra—never 'ave in all me life. Do it at onsh, I will.

[He moves across to the model's room at that peculiar broad gait so perfectly adjusted to his habits.

You quite understand me —couldn't bear to 'ave anything on me that wasn't mine.

[He passes out.]

ANN

Old fraud!

WELLWYN

"In" and "on." Mark my words, he'll restore the—bottles.

BERTLEY

But, my dear Wellwyn, that is stealing.

WELLWYN

We all have our discrepancies, Vicar.

ANN
Daddy! Discrepancies!

WELLWYN
Well, Ann, my theory is that as regards solids Timson's an Individualist, but as regards liquids he's a Socialist... or 'vice versa', according to taste.

BERTLEY
No, no, we mustn't joke about it. [Gravely.] I do think he should be spoken to.

WELLWYN
Yes, but not by me.

BERTLEY
Surely you're the proper person.

WELLWYN [Shaking his head]
It was my rum, Vicar. Look so personal.

[There sound a number of little tat-tat knocks.

WELLWYN
Isn't that the Professor's knock?

[While **ANN** sits down to make tea, he goes to the door and opens it. There, dressed in an ulster, stands a thin, clean-shaved **MAN**, with a little hollow sucked into either cheek, who, taking off a grey squash hat, discloses a majestically bald forehead, which completely dominates all that comes below it.

WELLWYN
Come in, Professor! So awfully good of you! You know Canon Bentley, I think?

CALWAY
Ah! How d'you do?

WELLWYN
Your opinion will be invaluable, Professor.

ANN
Tea, Professor Calway?

[They have assembled round the tea table.

CALWAY
Thank you; no tea; milk.

WELLWYN
Rum?

[He pours rum into **CALWAY's** milk.

CALWAY
A little-thanks!

[Turning to **ANN**.

You were going to show me some one you're trying to rescue, or something, I think.

ANN
Oh! Yes. He'll be here directly—simply perfect rotter.

CALWAY [Smiling]
Really! Ah! I think you said he was a congenital?

WELLWYN [With great interest]
What!

ANN [Low]
Daddy! [To **CALWAY**] Yes; I—I think that's what you call him.

CALWAY
Not old?

ANN
No; and quite healthy—a vagabond.

CALWAY [Sipping]
I see! Yes. Is it, do you think chronic unemployment with a vagrant tendency? Or would it be nearer the mark to say: Vagrancy—

WELLWYN
Pure! Oh! pure! Professor. Awfully human.

CALWAY [With a smile of knowledge]
Quite! And—er—

ANN [Breaking in]
Before he comes, there's another—

BERTLEY [Blandly]
Yes, when you came in, we were discussing what should be done with a man who drinks rum—

[**CALWAY** pauses in the act of drinking.

—that doesn't belong to him.

CALWAY
Really! Dipsomaniac?

BERTLEY
Well—perhaps you could tell us—drink certainly changing thine to mine. The Professor could see him, Wellwyn?

ANN [Rising]
Yes, do come and look at him, Professor Calway. He's in there.

[She points towards the model's room. **CALWAY** smiles deprecatingly.

ANN
No, really; we needn't open the door. You can see him through the glass. He's more than half—

CALWAY
Well, I hardly—

ANN
Oh! Do! Come on, Professor Calway! We must know what to do with him.

[**CALWAY** rises.

You can stand on a chair. It's all science.

[She draws **CALWAY** to the model's room, which is lighted by a glass panel in the top of the high door. **CANON BERTLEY** also rises and stands watching. **WELLWYN** hovers, torn between respect for science and dislike of espionage.

ANN [Drawing up a chair]
Come on!

CALWAY
Do you seriously wish me to?

ANN
Rather! It's quite safe; he can't see you.

CALWAY
But he might come out.

[**ANN** puts her back against the door. **CALWAY** mounts the chair dubiously, and raises his head cautiously, bending it more and more downwards.

ANN
Well?

CALWAY

He appears to be—sitting on the floor.

WELLWYN
Yes, that's all right!

[**BERTLEY** covers his lips.

CALWAY [To **ANN**—descending.]
By the look of his face, as far as one can see it, I should say there was a leaning towards mania. I know the treatment.

[There come three loud knocks on the door. **WELLWYN** and **ANN** exchange a glance of consternation.

ANN
Who's that?

WELLWYN
It sounds like Sir Thomas.

CALWAY
Sir Thomas Hoxton?

WELLWYN [Nodding]
Awfully sorry, Professor. You see, we—

CALWAY
Not at all. Only, I must decline to be involved in argument with him, please.

BERTLEY
He has experience. We might get his opinion, don't you think?

CALWAY
On a point of reform? A J.P.!

BERTLEY [Deprecating]
My dear Sir—we needn't take it.

[The three knocks resound with extraordinary fury.

ANN
You'd better open the door, Daddy.

[**WELLWYN** opens the door. **SIR THOMAS HOXTON** is disclosed in a fur overcoat and top hat. His square, well-coloured face is remarkable for a massive jaw, dominating all that comes above it. His Voice is resolute.

HOXTON
Afraid I didn't make myself heard.

WELLWYN
So good of you to come, Sir Thomas. Canon Bertley!

[They greet.

Professor Calway you know, I think.

HOXTON [Ominously]
I do.

[They almost greet. An awkward pause.

ANN [Blurting it out]
That old cabman I told you of's been drinking father's rum.

BERTLEY
We were just discussing what's to be done with him, Sir Thomas. One wants to do the very best, of course. The question of reform is always delicate.

CALWAY
I beg your pardon. There is no question here.

HOXTON [Abruptly]
Oh! Is he in the house?

ANN
In there.

HOXTON
Works for you, eh?

WELLWYN
Er—yes.

HOXTON
Let's have a look at him!

[An embarrassed pause.

BERTLEY
Well—the fact is, Sir Thomas—

CALWAY
When last under observation—

ANN
He was sitting on the floor.

WELLWYN
I don't want the old fellow to feel he's being made a show of. Disgusting to be spied at, Ann.

ANN
You can't, Daddy! He's drunk.

HOXTON
Never mind, Miss **WELLWYN**
Hundreds of these fellows before me in my time. [At **CALWAY**] The only thing is a sharp lesson!

CALWAY
I disagree. I've seen the man; what he requires is steady control, and the bobbins treatment.

[**WELLWYN** approaches them with fearful interest.

HOXTON
Not a bit of it! He wants one for his knob! Brace 'em up! It's the only thing.

BERTLEY
Personally, I think that if he were spoken to seriously

CALWAY
I cannot walk arm in arm with a crab!

HOXTON [Approaching **CALWAY**]
I beg your pardon?

CALWAY [Moving back a little]
You're moving backwards, Sir Thomas. I've told you before, convinced reactionaryism, in these days—

[There comes a single knock on the street door.

BERTLEY [Looking at his watch]
D'you know, I'm rather afraid this may be our young husband, Wellwyn. I told him half-past four.

WELLWYN
Oh! Ah! Yes.

[Going towards the **TWO REFORMERS**.

Shall we go into the house, Professor, and settle the question quietly while the Vicar sees a young man?

CALWAY [Pale with uncompleted statement, and gravitating insensibly in the direction indicated]
The merest sense of continuity—a simple instinct for order—

HOXTON [Following]
The only way to get order, sir, is to bring the disorderly up with a round turn.

[**CALWAY** turns to him in the doorway.
You people without practical experience—

CALWAY
If you'll listen to me a minute.

HOXTON
I can show you in a mo—

[They vanish through the door.

WELLWYN
I was afraid of it.

BERTLEY
The two points of view. Pleasant to see such keenness. I may want you, **WELLWYN**. And Ann perhaps had better not be present.

WELLWYN [Relieved]
Quite so! My dear!

[**ANN** goes reluctantly. **WELLWYN** opens the street door. The lamp outside has just been lighted, and, by its gleam, is seen the figure of **RORY MEGAN**, thin, pale, youthful. **ANN** turning at the door into the house gives him a long, inquisitive look, then goes.

WELLWYN
Is that Megan?

MEGAN
Yus.

WELLWYN
Come in.

[**MEGAN** comes in. There follows an awkward silence, during which **WELLWYN** turns up the light, then goes to the tea table and pours out a glass of tea and rum.

BERTLEY [Kindly]
Now, my boy, how is it that you and your wife are living apart like this?

MEGAN
I dunno.

BERTLEY
Well, if you don't, none of us are very likely to, are we?

MEGAN

That's what I thought, as I was comin' along.

WELLWYN [Twinkling]
Have some tea, Megan? [Handing him the glass.] What d'you think of her picture? 'Tisn't quite finished.

MEGAN [After scrutiny]
I seen her look like it—once.

WELLWYN
Good! When was that?

MEGAN [Stoically]
When she 'ad the measles.

[He drinks.]

WELLWYN [Ruminating]
I see—yes. I quite see feverish!

BERTLEY
My dear Wellwyn, let me—[To, **MEGAN**] Now, I hope you're willing to come together again, and to maintain her?

MEGAN
If she'll maintain me.

BERTLEY
Oh! but—I see, you mean you're in the same line of business?

MEGAN
Yus.

BERTLEY
And lean on each other. Quite so!

MEGAN
I leans on 'er mostly—with 'er looks.

BERTLEY
Indeed! Very interesting—that!

MEGAN
Yus. Sometimes she'll take 'arf a crown off of a toff.

[He looks at **WELLWYN**.

WELLWYN [Twinkling]

I apologise to you, Megan.

MEGAN [With a faint smile]
I could do with a bit more of it.

BERTLEY [Dubiously]
Yes! Yes! Now, my boy, I've heard you bet on horses.

MEGAN
No, I don't.

BERTLEY
Play cards, then? Come! Don't be afraid to acknowledge it.

MEGAN
When I'm 'ard up—yus.

BERTLEY
But don't you know that's ruination?

MEGAN
Depends. Sometimes I wins a lot.

BERTLEY
You know that's not at all what I mean. Come, promise me to give it up.

MEGAN
I dunno abaht that.

BERTLEY
Now, there's a good fellow. Make a big effort and throw the habit off!

MEGAN
Comes over me—same as it might over you.

BERTLEY
Over me! How do you mean, my boy?

MEGAN [With a look up]
To tork!

[**WELLWYN**, turning to the picture, makes a funny little noise.

BERTLEY [Maintaining his good humour]
A hit! But you forget, you know, to talk's my business. It's not yours to gamble.

MEGAN
You try sellin' flowers. If that ain't a—gamble

BERTLEY
I'm afraid we're wandering a little from the point. Husband and wife should be together. You were brought up to that. Your father and mother—

MEGAN
Never was.

WELLWYN [Turning from the picture]
The question is, Megan: Will you take your wife home? She's a good little soul.

MEGAN
She never let me know it.

[There is a feeble knock on the door.

WELLWYN
Well, now come. Here she is!

[He points to the door, and stands regarding **MEGAN** with his friendly smile.

MEGAN [With a gleam of responsiveness]
I might, perhaps, to please you, sir.

BERTLEY [Appropriating the gesture]
Capital, I thought we should get on in time.

MEGAN
Yus.

[**WELLWYN** opens the door. **MRS MEGAN** and **FERRAND** are revealed. They are about to enter, but catching sight of **MEGAN**, hesitate.

BERTLEY
Come in! Come in!

[**MRS MEGAN** enters stolidly. **FERRAND**, following, stands apart with an air of extreme detachment. **MEGAN**, after a quick glance at them both, remains unmoved. No one has noticed that the door of the model's room has been opened, and that the unsteady figure of old **TIMSON** is standing there.

BERTLEY [A little awkward in the presence of **FERRAND**—to the **MEGANS**]
This begins a new chapter. We won't improve the occasion. No need.

[**MEGAN**, turning towards his wife, makes her a gesture as if to say: "Here! let's get out of this!"

BENTLEY
Yes, yes, you'll like to get home at once—I know.

[He holds up his hand mechanically.

TIMSON
I forbids the banns.

BERTLEY [Startled]
Gracious!

TIMSON [Extremely unsteady]
Just cause and impejiment. There 'e stands.

[He points to **FERRAND**]

The crimson foreigner! The mockin' jay!

WELLWYN
Timson!

TIMSON
You're a gen'leman—I'm aweer o' that but I must speak the truth—[he waves his hand] an' shame the devil!

BERTLEY
Is this the rum—?

TIMSON [Struck by the word]
I'm a teetotaler.

WELLWYN
Timson, Timson!

TIMSON
Seein' as there's ladies present, I won't be conspicuous. [Moving away, and making for the door, he strikes against the dais, and mounts upon it.] But what I do say, is: He's no better than 'er and she's worse.

BERTLEY
This is distressing.

FERRAND [Calmly]
On my honour, Monsieur!

[**TIMSON** growls.

WELLWYN
Now, now, Timson!

TIMSON
That's all right. You're a gen'leman, an' I'm a gen'leman, but he ain't an' she ain't.

WELLWYN
We shall not believe you.

BERTLEY
No, no; we shall not believe you.

TIMSON [Heavily]
Very well, you doubts my word. Will it make any difference, Guv'nor, if I speaks the truth?

BERTLEY
No, certainly not—that is—of course, it will.

TIMSON
Well, then, I see 'em plainer than I see—

[Pointing at **BERTLEY**]

—the two of you.

WELLWYN
Be quiet, Timson!

BERTLEY
Not even her husband believes you.

MEGAN [Suddenly]
Don't I!

WELLWYN
Come, Megan, you can see the old fellow's in Paradise.

BERTLEY
Do you credit such a—such an object?

[He points at **TIMSON**, who seems falling asleep.

MEGAN
Naow!

[Unseen by anybody, **ANN** has returned.

BERTLEY
Well, then, my boy?

MEGAN

I seen 'em meself.

BERTLEY
Gracious! But just now you were will—

MEGAN [Sardonically]
There wasn't nothing against me honour, then. Now you've took it away between you, cumin' aht with it like this. I don't want no more of 'er, and I'll want a good deal more of 'im; as 'e'll soon find.

[He jerks his chin at **FERRAND**, turns slowly on his heel, and goes out into the street.

[There follows a profound silence.

ANN
What did I say, Daddy? Utter! All three.

[Suddenly alive to her presence, they all turn.

TIMSON [Waking up and looking round him]
Well, p'raps I'd better go.

[Assisted by **WELLWYN** he lurches gingerly off the dais towards the door, which **WELLWYN** holds open for him.

TIMSON [Mechanically]
Where to, sir?

[Receiving no answer he passes out, touching his hat; and the door is closed.

WELLWYN
Ann!

[**ANN** goes back whence she came.]

[**BERTLEY**, steadily regarding **MRS MEGAN**, who has put her arm up in front of her face, beckons to **FERRAND**, and the young man comes gravely forward.

BERTLEY
Young people, this is very dreadful.

[**MRS MEGAN** lowers her arm a little, and looks at him over it.

Very sad!

MRS MEGAN [Dropping her arm]
Megan's no better than what I am.

BERTLEY

Come, come! Here's your home broken up!

[MRS MEGAN smiles. Shaking his head gravely.

Surely-surely-you mustn't smile.

[MRS MEGAN becomes tragic.

That's better. Now, what is to be done?

FERRAND
Believe me, Monsieur, I greatly regret.

BERTLEY
I'm glad to hear it.

FERRAND
If I had foreseen this disaster.

BERTLEY
Is that your only reason for regret?

FERRAND [With a little bow]
Any reason that you wish, Monsieur. I will do my possible.

MRS MEGAN
I could get an unfurnished room if—

[She slides her eyes round at WELLWYN

—I 'ad the money to furnish it.

BERTLEY
But suppose I can induce your husband to forgive you, and take you back?

MRS MEGAN [Shaking her head]
'E'd 'it me.

BERTLEY
I said to forgive.

MRS MEGAN
That wouldn't make no difference.

[With a flash at **BERTLEY**.

An' I ain't forgiven him!

BERTLEY
That is sinful.

MRS MEGAN
I'm a Catholic.

BERTLEY
My good child, what difference does that make?

FERRAND
Monsieur, if I might interpret for her.

[**BERTLEY** silences him with a gesture.

MRS MEGAN [Sliding her eyes towards **WELLWYN**]
If I 'ad the money to buy some fresh stock.

BERTLEY
Yes; yes; never mind the money. What I want to find in you both, is repentance.

MRS MEGAN [With a flash up at him]
I can't get me livin' off of repentin'.

BERTLEY
Now, now! Never say what you know to be wrong.

FERRAND
Monsieur, her soul is very simple.

BERTLEY [Severely]
I do not know, sir, that we shall get any great assistance from your views. In fact, one thing is clear to me, she must discontinue your acquaintanceship at once.

FERRAND
Certainly, Monsieur. We have no serious intentions.

BERTLEY
All the more shame to you, then!

FERRAND
Monsieur, I see perfectly your point of view. It is very natural.

[He bows and is silent.]

MRS MEGAN
I don't want'im hurt'cos o' me. Megan'll get his mates to belt him—bein' foreign like he is.

BERTLEY

Yes, never mind that. It's you I'm thinking of.

MRS MEGAN
I'd sooner they'd hit me.

WELLWYN [Suddenly]
Well said, my child!

MRS MEGAN
'Twasn't his fault.

FERRAND [Without irony—to **WELLWYN**]
I cannot accept that Monsieur. The blame—it is all mine.

ANN [Entering suddenly from the house]
Daddy, they're having an awful—!

[The voices of **PROFESSOR CALWAY** and **SIR THOMAS HOXTON** are distinctly heard.

CALWAY
The question is a much wider one, Sir Thomas.

HOXTON
As wide as you like, you'll never—

[**WELLWYN** pushes **ANN** back into the house and closes the door behind her. The voices are still faintly heard arguing on the threshold.

BERTLEY
Let me go in here a minute, Wellyn. I must finish speaking to her.

[He motions **MRS MEGAN** towards the model's room.

We can't leave the matter thus.

FERRAND [Suavely]
Do you desire my company, Monsieur?

[**BERTLEY**, with a prohibitive gesture of his hand, shepherds the reluctant **MRS MEGAN** into the model's room.

WELLWYN [Sorrowfully]
You shouldn't have done this, Ferrand. It wasn't the square thing.

FERRAND [With dignity]
Monsieur, I feel that I am in the wrong. It was stronger than me.

[As he speaks, **SIR THOMAS HOXTON** and **PROFESSOR CALWAY** enter from the house. In the dim light, and the full cry of argument, they do not notice the figures at the fire. **SIR THOMAS HOXTON** leads towards the street door.

HOXTON
No, Sir, I repeat, if the country once commits itself to your views of reform, it's as good as doomed.

CALWAY
I seem to have heard that before, Sir Thomas. And let me say at once that your hitty-missy cart-load of bricks regime—

HOXTON
Is a deuced sight better, sir, than your grand-motherly methods. What the old fellow wants is a shock! With all this socialistic molly-coddling, you're losing sight of the individual.

CALWAY [Swiftly]
You, sir, with your "devil take the hindmost," have never even seen him.

[**SIR THOMAS HOXTON**, throwing back a gesture of disgust, steps out into the night, and falls heavily **PROFESSOR CALWAY**, hastening to his rescue, falls more heavily still.

[**TIMSON**, momentarily roused from slumber on the doorstep, sits up.

HOXTON [Struggling to his knees]
Damnation!

CALWAY [Sitting]
How simultaneous!

[**WELLWYN** and **FERRAND** approach hastily.

FERRAND [Pointing to **TIMSON**]
Monsieur, it was true, it seems. They had lost sight of the individual.

[A **POLICEMAN** has appeared under the street lamp. He picks up Hoxton's hat.

CONSTABLE
Anything wrong, sir?

HOXTON [Recovering his feet]
Wrong? Great Scott! Constable! Why do you let things lie about in the street like this? Look here, Wellyn!

[They all scrutinize **TIMSON**.

WELLWYN
It's only the old fellow whose reform you were discussing.

HOXTON
How did he come here?

CONSTABLE
Drunk, sir.

[Ascertaining **TIMSON** to be in the street.

Just off the premises, by good luck. Come along, father.

TIMSON [Assisted to his feet-drowsily]
Cert'nly, by no means; take my arm.

[They move from the doorway. **HOXTON** and **CALWAY** re-enter, and go towards the fire.

ANN [Entering from the house]
What's happened?

CALWAY
Might we have a brush?

HOXTON [Testily]
Let it dry!

[He moves to the fire and stands before it. **PROFESSOR CALWAY** following stands a little behind him.
ANN returning begins to brush the Professor's sleeve.

WELLWYN [Turning from the door, where he has stood looking after the receding **TIMSON**]
Poor old Timson!

FERRAND [Softly]
Must be philosopher, Monsieur! They will but run him in a little.

[From the model's room **MRS MEGAN** has come out, shepherded by **CANON BERTLEY**.

BERTLEY
Let's see, your Christian name is—.

MRS MEGAN
Guinevere.

BERTLEY
Oh! Ah! Ah! Ann, take Gui—take our little friend into the study a minute: I am going to put her into service. We shall make a new woman of her, yet.

ANN [Handing **CANON BERTLEY** the brush, and turning to **MRS MEGAN**]
Come on!

[She leads into the house, and **MRS MEGAN** follows Stolidly.

BERTLEY [Brushing **CALWAY'S** back]
Have you fallen?

CALWAY
Yes.

BERTLEY
Dear me! How was that?

HOXTON
That old ruffian drunk on the doorstep. Hope they'll give him a sharp dose! These rag-tags!

[He looks round, and his angry eyes light by chance on **FERRAND**.

FERRAND [With his eyes on **HOXTON**—softly]
Monsieur, something tells me it is time I took the road again.

WELLWYN [Fumbling out a sovereign]
Take this, then!

FERRAND [Refusing the coin]
Non, Monsieur. To abuse 'ospitality is not in my character.

BERTLEY
We must not despair of anyone.

HOXTON
Who talked of despairing? Treat him, as I say, and you'll see!

CALWAY
The interest of the State—

HOXTON
The interest of the individual citizen sir—

BERTLEY
Come! A little of both, a little of both!

[They resume their brushing.

FERRAND
You are now debarrassed of us three, Monsieur. I leave you instead—these sirs.

[He points.

'Au revoir, Monsieur'!

[Motioning towards the fire.

'Appy New Year!

[He slips quietly out. **WELLWYN**, turning, contemplates the three reformers. They are all now brushing away, scratching each other's backs, and gravely hissing. As he approaches them, they speak with a certain unanimity.

HOXTON
My theory—!

CALWAY
My theory—!

BERTLEY
My theory—!

[They stop surprised. **WELLWYN** makes a gesture of discomfort, as they speak again with still more unanimity.

HOXTON
My—!

CALWAY
My—!

BERTLEY
My—!

[They stop in greater surprise. The stage is blotted dark.

Curtain.

ACT III

It is the first of April—a white spring day of gleams and driving showers. The street door of Wellwyn's studio stands wide open, and, past it, in the street, the wind is whirling bits of straw and paper bags. Through the door can be seen the butt end of a stationary furniture van with its flap let down. To this van three humble-men in shirt sleeves and aprons, are carrying out the contents of the studio. The hissing samovar, the tea-pot, the sugar, and the nearly empty decanter of rum stand on the low round table in the fast-being-gutted room. **WELLWYN** in his ulster and soft hat, is squatting on the little stool in front of the blazing fire, staring into it, and smoking a hand-made cigarette. He has a moulting air. Behind him the humble-men pass, embracing busts and other articles of vertu.

CHIEF H'MAN [Stopping, and standing in the attitude of expectation]

We've about pinched this little lot, sir. Shall we take the—reservoir?

[He indicates the samovar.

WELLWYN
Ah!

[Abstractedly feeling in his pockets, and finding coins.

Thanks—thanks—heavy work, I'm afraid.

H'MAN [Receiving the coins—a little surprised and a good deal pleased]
Thank'ee, sir. Much obliged, I'm sure. We'll 'ave to come back for this.

[He gives the dais a vigorous push with his foot]

Not a fixture, as I understand. Perhaps you'd like us to leave these 'ere for a bit.

[He indicates the tea things.

WELLWYN
Ah! do.

[The humble-men go out. There is the sound of horses being started, and the butt end of the van disappears. **WELLWYN** stays on his stool, smoking and brooding over the fare. The open doorway is darkened by a figure. **CANON BERTLEY** is standing there.

BERTLEY
WELLWYN!

[**WELLWYN** turns and rises.

It's ages since I saw you. No idea you were moving. This is very dreadful.

WELLWYN
Yes, Ann found this—too exposed. That tall house in Flight Street—we're going there. Seventh floor.

BERTLEY
Lift?

[**WELLWYN** shakes his head.

BERTLEY
Dear me! No lift? Fine view, no doubt.

[**WELLWYN** nods.

You'll be greatly missed.

WELLWYN

So Ann thinks. Vicar, what's become of that little flower-seller I was painting at Christmas? You took her into service.

BERTLEY

Not we—exactly! Some dear friends of ours. Painful subject!

WELLWYN

Oh!

BERTLEY

Yes. She got the footman into trouble.

WELLWYN

Did she, now?

BERTLEY

Disappointing. I consulted with Calway, and he advised me to try a certain institution. We got her safely in—excellent place; but, d'you know, she broke out three weeks ago. And since— I've heard—

[He holds his hands up]

—hopeless, I'm afraid—quite!

WELLWYN

I thought I saw her last night. You can't tell me her address, I suppose?

BERTLEY [Shaking his head]

The husband too has quite passed out of my ken. He betted on horses, you remember. I'm sometimes tempted to believe there's nothing for some of these poor folk but to pray for death.

[**ANN** has entered from the house. Her hair hangs from under a knitted cap. She wears a white wool jersey, and a loose silk scarf.

BERTLEY

Ah! Ann. I was telling your father of that poor little Mrs. Megan.

ANN

Is she dead?

BERTLEY

Worse I fear. By the way—what became of her accomplice?

ANN

We haven't seen him since.

[She looks searchingly at **WELLWYN**.

At least—have you—Daddy?

WELLWYN [Rather hurt]
No, my dear; I have not.

BERTLEY
And the—old gentleman who drank the rum?

ANN
He got fourteen days. It was the fifth time.

BERTLEY
Dear me!

ANN
When he came out he got more drunk than ever. Rather a score for Professor Calway, wasn't it?

BERTLEY
I remember. He and Sir Thomas took a kindly interest in the old fellow.

ANN
Yes, they fell over him. The Professor got him into an Institution.

BERTLEY
Indeed!

ANN
He was perfectly sober all the time he was there.

WELLWYN
My dear, they only allow them milk.

ANN
Well, anyway, he was reformed.

WELLWYN
Ye-yes!

ANN [Terribly]
Daddy! You've been seeing him!

WELLWYN [With dignity]
My dear, I have not.

ANN
How do you know, then?

WELLWYN
Came across Sir Thomas on the Embankment yesterday; told me old Timso—had been had up again for sitting down in front of a brewer's dray.

ANN
Why?

WELLWYN
Well, you see, as soon as he came out of the what d'you call 'em, he got drunk for a week, and it left him in low spirits.

BERTLEY
Do you mean he deliberately sat down, with the intention—of—er?

WELLWYN
Said he was tired of life, but they didn't believe him.

ANN
Rather a score for Sir Thomas! I suppose he'd told the Professor? What did he say?

WELLWYN
Well, the Professor said

[With a quick glance at **BERTLEY**.

he felt there was nothing for some of these poor devils but a lethal chamber.

BERTLEY [Shocked]
Did he really!

[He has not yet caught **WELLWYN'** s glance.

WELLWYN
And Sir Thomas agreed. Historic occasion. And you, Vicar H'm!

[**BERTLEY** winces.

ANN [To herself]
Well, there isn't.

BERTLEY
And yet! Some good in the old fellow, no doubt, if one could put one's finger on it.

[Preparing to go.

You'll let us know, then, when you're settled. What was the address?

[**WELLWYN** takes out and hands him a card.

Ah! yes. Good-bye, Ann. Good-bye, Wellwyn.

[The wind blows his hat along the street.

What a wind!

[He goes, pursuing.

ANN [Who has eyed the card askance]
Daddy, have you told those other two where we're going?

WELLWYN
Which other two, my dear?

ANN
The Professor and Sir Thomas.

WELLWYN
Well, Ann, naturally I—

ANN [Jumping on to the dais with disgust]
Oh, dear! When I'm trying to get you away from all this atmosphere. I don't so much mind the Vicar knowing, because he's got a weak heart—

[She jumps off again.

WELLWYN [To himself]
Seventh floor! I felt there was something.

ANN [Preparing to go]
I'm going round now. But you must stay here till the van comes back. And don't forget you tipped the men after the first load.

WELLWYN
Oh! Yes, yes. [Uneasily.] Good sorts they look, those fellows!

ANN [Scrutinising him]
What have you done?

WELLWYN
Nothing, my dear, really—!

ANN
What?

WELLWYN
I—I rather think I may have tipped them twice.

ANN [Drily]

Daddy! If it is the first of April, it's not necessary to make a fool of oneself. That's the last time you ever do these ridiculous things.

[**WELLWYN** eyes her askance.

I'm going to see that you spend your money on yourself. You needn't look at me like that! I mean to. As soon as I've got you away from here, and all—these—

WELLWYN

Don't rub it in, Ann!

ANN

[Giving him a sudden hug—then going to the door—with a sort of triumph.] Deeds, not words, Daddy!

[She goes out, and the wind catching her scarf blows it out beneath her firm young chin. **WELLWYN** returning to the fire, stands brooding, and gazing at his extinct cigarette.

WELLWYN [To himself]

Bad lot—low type! No method! No theory!

[In the open doorway appear **FERRAND** and **MRS MEGAN.** They stand, unseen, looking at him. **FERRAND** is more ragged, if possible, than on Christmas Eve. His chin and cheeks are clothed in a reddish golden beard. **MRS MEGAN'S** dress is not so woe-begone, but her face is white, her eyes dark-circled. They whisper. She slips back into the shadow of the doorway. **WELLWYN** turns at the sound, and stares at **FERRAND** in amazement.

FERRAND [Advancing]

Enchanted to see you, Monsieur.

[He looks round the empty room.

You are leaving?

WELLWYN [Nodding—then taking the young man's hand]

How goes it?

FERRAND [Displaying himself, simply]

As you see, Monsieur. I have done of my best. It still flies from me.

WELLWYN [Sadly—as if against his will]

Ferrand, it will always fly.

[The young foreigner shivers suddenly from head to foot; then controls himself with a great effort.

FERRAND

Don't say that, Monsieur! It is too much the echo of my heart.

WELLWYN
Forgive me! I didn't mean to pain you.

FERRAND [Drawing nearer the fire]
That old cabby, Monsieur, you remember—they tell me, he nearly succeeded to gain happiness the other day.

[**WELLWYN** nods.

FERRAND
And those Sirs, so interested in him, with their theories? He has worn them out? [WELLWYN nods.] That goes without saying. And now they wish for him the lethal chamber.

WELLWYN [Startled]
How did you know that?

[There is silence.

FERRAND [Staring into the fire]
Monsieur, while I was on the road this time I fell ill of a fever. It seemed to me in my illness that I saw the truth—how I was wasting in this world—I would never be good for any one—nor any one for me—all would go by, and I never of it—fame, and fortune, and peace, even the necessities of life, ever mocking me.

[He draws closer to the fire, spreading his fingers to the flame. And while he is speaking, through the doorway **MRS MEGAN** creeps in to listen.

FERRAND [Speaking on into the fire]
And I saw, Monsieur, so plain, that I should be vagabond all my days, and my days short, I dying in the end the death of a dog. I saw it all in my fever— clear as that flame—there was nothing for us others, but the herb of death.

[**WELLWYN** takes his arm and presses it]
And so, Monsieur, I wished to die. I told no one of my fever. I lay out on the ground—it was verree cold. But they would not let me die on the roads of their parishes—they took me to an Institution, Monsieur, I looked in their eyes while I lay there, and I saw more clear than the blue heaven that they thought it best that I should die, although they would not let me. Then Monsieur, naturally my spirit rose, and I said: "So much the worse for you. I will live a little more." One is made like that! Life is sweet, Monsieur.

WELLWYN
Yes, Ferrand; Life is sweet.

FERRAND
That little girl you had here, Monsieur

[**WELLWYN** nods.

—in her too there is something of wild-savage. She must have joy of life. I have seen her since I came back. She has embraced the life of joy. It is not quite the same thing.

[He lowers his voice.

She is lost, Monsieur, as a stone that sinks in water. I can see, if she cannot.

[As **WELLWYN** makes a movement of distress.

Oh! I am not to blame for that, Monsieur. It had well begun before I knew her.

WELLWYN
Yes, yes—I was afraid of it, at the time.

[**MRS MEGAN** turns silently, and slips away.

FEERRAND
I do my best for her, Monsieur, but look at me! Besides, I am not good for her—it is not good for simple souls to be with those who see things clear. For the great part of mankind, to see anything—is fatal.

WELLWYN
Even for you, it seems.

FERRAND
No, Monsieur. To be so near to death has done me good; I shall not lack courage any more till the wind blows on my grave. Since I saw you, Monsieur, I have been in three Institutions. They are palaces. One may eat upon the floor—though it is true—for Kings—they eat too much of skilly there. One little thing they lack—those palaces. It is understanding of the 'uman heart. In them tame birds pluck wild birds naked.

WELLWYN
They mean well.

FERRAND
Ah! Monsieur, I am loafer, waster—what you like—for all that [bitterly] poverty is my only crime. If I were rich, should I not be simply veree original, 'ighly respected, with soul above commerce, travelling to see the world? And that young girl, would she not be "that charming ladee," "veree chic, you know!" And the old Tims—good old-fashioned gentleman—drinking his liquor well. Eh! bien—what are we now? Dark beasts, despised by all. That is life, Monsieur.

[He stares into the fire.

WELLWYN
We're our own enemies, Ferrand. I can afford it—you can't. Quite true!

FERRAND [Earnestly]
Monsieur, do you know this? You are the sole being that can do us good—we hopeless ones.

WELLWYN [Shaking his head]
Not a bit of it; I'm hopeless too.

FERRAND [Eagerly]
Monsieur, it is just that. You understand. When we are with you we feel something—here—[he touches his heart.] If I had one prayer to make, it would be, Good God, give me to understand! Those sirs, with their theories, they can clean our skins and chain our 'abits—that soothes for them the aesthetic sense; it gives them too their good little importance. But our spirits they cannot touch, for they nevare understand. Without that, Monsieur, all is dry as a parched skin of orange.

WELLWYN
Don't be so bitter. Think of all the work they do!

FERRAND
Monsieur, of their industry I say nothing. They do a good work while they attend with their theories to the sick and the tame old, and the good unfortunate deserving. Above all to the little children. But, Monsieur, when all is done, there are always us hopeless ones. What can they do with me, Monsieur, with that girl, or with that old man? Ah! Monsieur, we, too, 'ave our qualities, we others—it wants you courage to undertake a career like mine, or like that young girl's. We wild ones—we know a thousand times more of life than ever will those sirs. They waste their time trying to make rooks white. Be kind to us if you will, or let us alone like Mees Ann, but do not try to change our skins. Leave us to live, or leave us to die when we like in the free air. If you do not wish of us, you have but to shut your pockets and—your doors—we shall die the faster.

WELLWYN [With agitation]
But that, you know—we can't do—now can we?

FERRAND
If you cannot, how is it our fault? The harm we do to others—is it so much? If I am criminal, dangerous—shut me up! I would not pity myself—nevare. But we in whom something moves— like that flame, Monsieur, that cannot keep still—we others—we are not many—that must have motion in our lives, do not let them make us prisoners, with their theories, because we are not like them—it is life itself they would enclose!

[He draws up his tattered figure, then bending over the fire again.

I ask your pardon; I am talking. If I could smoke, Monsieur!

[**WELLWYN** hands him a tobacco pouch; and he rolls a cigarette with his yellow-Stained fingers.

FERRAND
The good God made me so that I would rather walk a whole month of nights, hungry, with the stars, than sit one single day making round business on an office stool! It is not to my advantage. I cannot help it that I am a vagabond. What would you have? It is stronger than me.

[He looks suddenly at **WELLWYN**.

Monsieur, I say to you things I have never said.

WELLWYN [Quietly]
Go on, go on.

[There is silence.]

FERRAND [Suddenly]
Monsieur! Are you really English? The English are so civilised.

WELLWYN
And am I not?

FERRAND
You treat me like a brother.

[**WELLWYN** has turned towards the street door at a sound of feet, and the clamour of voices.

TIMSON [From the street]
Take her in 'ere. I knows 'im.

[Through the open doorway come a **POLICE CONSTABLE** and a **LOAFER**, bearing between them the limp white faced form of **MRS MEGAN**, hatless and with drowned hair, enveloped in the policeman's waterproof. Some curious persons bring up the rear, jostling in the doorway, among whom is **TIMSON** carrying in his hands the policeman's dripping waterproof leg pieces.

FERRAND [Starting forward]
Monsieur, it is that little girl!

WELLWYN
What's happened? Constable! What's happened!

[The **CONSTABLE** and **LOAFER** have laid the body down on the dais; with **WELLWYN** and **FERRAND** they stand bending over her.

CONSTABLE
'Tempted sooicide, sir; but she hadn't been in the water 'arf a minute when I got hold of her.

[He bends lower.

Can't understand her collapsin' like this.

WELLWYN [Feeling her heart]
I don't feel anything.

FERRAND [In a voice sharpened by emotion]
Let me try, Monsieur.

CONSTABLE. [Touching his arm]
You keep off, my lad.

WELLWYN
No, constable—let him. He's her friend.

CONSTABLE [Releasing **FERRAND**—to the **LOAFER**]
Here you! Cut off for a doctor-sharp now!

[He pushes back the curious persons.

Now then, stand away there, please—we can't have you round the body. Keep back—Clear out, now!

[He slowly moves them back, and at last shepherds them through the door and shuts it on them, **TIMSON** being last.

FERRAND
The rum!

[**WELLWYN** fetches the decanter. With the little there is left **FERRAND** chafes the girl's hands and forehead, and pours some between her lips. But there is no response from the inert body.

FERRAND
Her soul is still away, Monsieur!

[**WELLWYN**, seizing the decanter, pours into it tea and boiling water.

CONSTABLE
It's never drownin', sir—her head was hardly under; I was on to her like knife.

FERRAND [Rubbing her feet]
She has not yet her philosophy, Monsieur; at the beginning they often try. If she is dead!

[In a voice of awed rapture.

What fortune!

CONSTABLE [With puzzled sadness]
True enough, sir—that! We'd just begun to know 'er. If she 'as been taken—her best friends couldn't wish 'er better.

WELLWYN [Applying the decanter to her dips]
Poor little thing! I'll try this hot tea.

FERRAND [Whispering]
'La mort—le grand ami!'

WELLWYN

Look! Look at her! She's coming round!

[A faint tremor passes over **MRS MEGAN'S** body. He again applies the hot drink to her mouth. She stirs and gulps.

CONSTABLE [With intense relief]
That's brave! Good lass! She'll pick up now, sir.

[Then, seeing that **TIMSON** and the curious persons have again opened the door, he drives them out, and stands with his back against it. **MRS MEGAN** comes to herself.

WELLWYN [Sitting on the dais and supporting her—as if to a child]
There you are, my dear. There, there—better now! That's right. Drink a little more of this tea.

[**MRS MEGAN** drinks from the decanter.

FERRAND [Rising]
Bring her to the fire, Monsieur.

[They take her to the fire and seat her on the little stool. From the moment of her restored animation **FERRAND** has resumed his air of cynical detachment, and now stands apart with arms folded, watching.

WELLWYN
Feeling better, my child?

MRS MEGAN
Yes.

WELLWYN
That's good. That's good. Now, how was it? Um?

MRS MEGAN
I dunno.

[She shivers.

I was standin' here just now when you was talkin', and when I heard 'im, it cam' over me to do it—like.

WELLWYN
Ah, yes I know.

MRS MEGAN
I didn't seem no good to meself nor any one. But when I got in the water, I didn't want to any more. It was cold in there.

WELLWYN
Have you been having such a bad time of it?

MRS MEGAN

Yes. And listenin' to him upset me.

[She signs with her head at **FERRAND**.

I feel better now I've been in the water.

[She smiles and shivers.

WELLWYN

There, there! Shivery? Like to walk up and down a little?

[They begin walking together up and down.

WELLWYN

Beastly when your head goes under?

MRS MEGAN

Yes. It frightened me. I thought I wouldn't come up again.

WELLWYN

I know—sort of world without end, wasn't it? What did you think of, um?

MRS MEGAN

I wished I 'adn't jumped—an' I thought of my baby— that died—and—[in a rather surprised voice] and I thought of d-dancin'.

[Her mouth quivers, her face puckers, she gives a choke and a little sob.

WELLWYN [Stopping and stroking her]
There, there—there!

[For a moment her face is buried in his sleeve, then she recovers herself.

MRS MEGAN

Then 'e got hold o' me, an' pulled me out.

WELLWYN

Ah! what a comfort—um?

MRS MEGAN

Yes. The water got into me mouth.

[They walk again.

I wouldn't have gone to do it but for him.

[She looks towards **FERRAND**.

His talk made me feel all funny, as if people wanted me to.

WELLWYN
My dear child! Don't think such things! As if anyone would—!

MRS MEGAN [Stolidly]
I thought they did. They used to look at me so sometimes, where I was before I ran away—I couldn't stop there, you know.

WELLWYN
Too cooped-up?

MRS MEGAN
Yes. No life at all, it wasn't—not after sellin' flowers, I'd rather be doin' what I am.

WELLWYN
Ah! Well-it's all over, now! How d'you feel—eh? Better?

MRS MEGAN
Yes. I feels all right now.

[She sits up again on the little stool before the fire.

WELLWYN
No shivers, and no aches; quite comfy?

MRS MEGAN
Yes.

WELLWYN
That's a blessing. All well, now, Constable—thank you!

CONSTABLE [Who has remained discreetly apart at the door-cordially]
First rate, sir! That's capital!

[He approaches and scrutinises **MRS MEGAN**]

Right as rain, eh, my girl?

MRS MEGAN [Shrinking a little]
Yes.

CONSTABLE
That's fine. Then I think perhaps, for 'er sake, sir, the sooner we move on and get her a change o' clothin', the better.

WELLWYN

Oh! don't bother about that—I'll send round for my daughter—we'll manage for her here.

CONSTABLE
Very kind of you, I'm sure, sir. But [with embarrassment] she seems all right. She'll get every attention at the station.

WELLWYN
But I assure you, we don't mind at all; we'll take the greatest care of her.

CONSTABLE [Still more embarrassed]
Well, sir, of course, I'm thinkin' of—I'm afraid I can't depart from the usual course.

WELLWYN [Sharply]
What! But-oh! No! No! That'll be all right, Constable! That'll be all right! I assure you.

CONSTABLE [With more decision]
I'll have to charge her, sir.

WELLWYN
Good God! You don't mean to say the poor little thing has got to be—

CONSTABLE [Consulting with him]
Well, sir, we can't get over the facts, can we? There it is! You know what sooicide amounts to— it's an awkward job.

WELLWYN [Calming himself with an effort]
But look here, Constable, as a reasonable man—This poor wretched little girl—you know what that life means better than anyone! Why! It's to her credit to try and jump out of it!

[The **CONSTABLE** shakes his head.

WELLWYN
You said yourself her best friends couldn't wish her better!

[Dropping his voice still more.

Everybody feels it! The Vicar was here a few minutes ago saying the very same thing—the Vicar, Constable!

[The **CONSTABLE** shakes his head.

Ah! now, look here, I know something of her. Nothing can be done with her. We all admit it. Don't you see? Well, then hang it—you needn't go and make fools of us all by—

FERRAND
Monsieur, it is the first of April.

CONSTABLE [With a sharp glance at him]

Can't neglect me duty, sir; that's impossible.

WELLWYN
Look here! She—slipped. She's been telling me. Come, Constable, there's a good fellow. May be the making of her, this.

CONSTABLE. I quite appreciate your good 'eart, sir, an' you make it very 'ard for me—but, come now! I put it to you as a gentleman, would you go back on yer duty if you was me?

[**WELLWYN** raises his hat, and plunges his fingers through and through his hair.

WELLWYN
Well! God in heaven! Of all the d—d topsy—turvy—! Not a soul in the world wants her alive—and now she's to be prosecuted for trying to be where everyone wishes her.

CONSTABLE. Come, sir, come! Be a man!

[Throughout all this **MRS. MEGAN** has sat stolidly before the fire, but as **FERRAND** suddenly steps forward she looks up at him.

FERRAND
Do not grieve, Monsieur! This will give her courage. There is nothing that gives more courage than to see the irony of things.

[He touches **MRS MEGAN'S** shoulder]

Go, my child; it will do you good.

[**MRS MEGAN** rises, and looks at him dazedly.

CONSTABLE. [Coming forward, and taking her by the hand]
That's my good lass. Come along! We won't hurt you.

MRS MEGAN
I don't want to go. They'll stare at me.

CONSTABLE. [Comforting]
Not they! I'll see to that.

WELLWYN [Very upset]
Take her in a cab, Constable, if you must —for God's sake!

[He pulls out a shilling.

Here!

CONSTABLE [Taking the shilling]
I will, sir, certainly. Don't think I want to—

WELLWYN

No, no, I know. You're a good sort.

CONSTABLE [Comfortable]

Don't you take on, sir. It's her first try; they won't be hard on 'er. Like as not only bind 'er over in her own recogs. not to do it again. Come, my dear.

MRS MEGAN [Trying to free herself from the policeman's cloak]

I want to take this off. It looks so funny.

[As she speaks the door is opened by **ANN**; behind whom is dimly seen the form of old **TIMSON**, still heading the curious persons.

ANN

[Looking from one to the other in amazement.] What is it? What's happened? Daddy!

FERRAND [Out of the silence]

It is nothing, Ma'moiselle! She has failed to drown herself. They run her in a little.

WELLWYN

Lend her your jacket, my dear; she'll catch her death.

[**ANN**, feeling **MRS MEGAN'S** arm, strips of her jacket, and helps her into it without a word.

CONSTABLE [Donning his cloak]

Thank you. Miss—very good of you, I'm sure.

MRS MEGAN [Mazed]

It's warm!

[She gives them all a last half-smiling look, and Passes with the **CONSTABLE** through the doorway.

FERRAND

That makes the third of us, Monsieur. We are not in luck. To wish us dead, it seems, is easier than to let us die.

[He looks at **ANN**, who is standing with her eyes fixed on her father. **WELLWYN** has taken from his pocket a visiting card.

WELLWYN [To **FERRAND**]

Here quick; take this, run after her! When they've done with her tell her to come to us.

FERRAND [Taking the card, and reading the address]

"No. 7, Haven House, Flight Street!" Rely on me, Monsieur—I will bring her myself to call on you. 'Au revoir, mon bon Monsieur'!

[He bends over **WELLWYN'S** hand; then, with a bow to **ANN** goes out; his tattered figure can be seen through the window, passing in the wind. **WELLWYN** turns back to the fire. The figure of **TIMSON** advances into the doorway, no longer holding in either hand a waterproof leg-piece.

TIMSON [In a croaky voice]
Sir!

WELLWYN
What—you, Timson?

TIMSON
On me larst legs, sir. 'Ere! You can see 'em for yerself! Shawn't trouble yer long....

WELLWYN [After a long and desperate stare]
Not now—Timson not now! Take this!

[He takes out another card, and hands it to **TIMSON**.

Some other time.

TIMSON [Taking the card]
Yer new address! You are a gen'leman.

[He lurches slowly away.

[**ANN** shuts the street door and sets her back against it. The rumble of the approaching van is heard outside. It ceases.

ANN [In a fateful voice]
Daddy!

[They stare at each other]

Do you know what you've done? Given your card to those six rotters.

WELLWYN [With a blank stare]
Six?

ANN [Staring round the naked room]
What was the good of this?

WELLWYN [Following her eyes—very gravely]
Ann! It is stronger than me.

[Without a word **ANN** opens the door, and walks straight out. With a heavy sigh, **WELLWYN** sinks down on the little stool before the fire. The **THREE HUMBLE-MEN** come in.

CHIEF HUMBLE-MAN [In an attitude of expectation]

This is the larst of it, sir.

WELLWYN
Oh! Ah! yes!

[He gives them money; then something seems to strike him, and he exhibits certain signs of vexation. Suddenly he recovers, looks from one to the other, and then at the tea things. A faint smile comes on his face.

WELLWYN
You can finish the decanter.

[He goes out in haste.

CHIEF HUMBLE-MAN [Clinking the coins]
Third time of arskin'! April fool! Not 'arf! Good old pigeon!

SECOND HUMBLE-MAN
'Uman being, I call 'im.

CHIEF HUMBLE-MAN [Taking the three glasses from the last packing-case, and pouring very equally into them]
That's right. Tell you wot, I'd never 'a touched this unless 'e'd told me to, I wouldn't—not with 'im.

SECOND HUMBLE-MAN
Ditto to that! This is a bit of orl right!

[Raising his glass.
Good luck!

THIRD HUMBLE-MAN
Same 'ere!

[Simultaneously they place their lips smartly against the liquor, and at once let fall their faces and their glasses.

CHIEF HUMBLE-MAN [With great solemnity]
Crikey! Bill! Tea! .....'E's got us!

[The stage is blotted dark.

Curtain.

John Galsworthy – A Short Biography

John Galsworthy, eldest son of John Galsworthy (1817-1904), a solicitor and company director of Old Jewry, London, and Blanche Bailey (1835-1915), daughter of Charles Bartleet, a needlemaker in Redditch. His father's ancestors originated in Wembury, near Plymouth in England, and Galsworthy, for whom family origins were of significant importance, maintained a close connection with Devon. His more immediate family were considerably wealthy and well established in the shipping industry, and owned a fine estate in Kingston-upon-Thames called Parkfield, where Galsworthy was born on the 14th August 1867. At the age of nine he began education at Saugeen, a Bournemouth preparatory school, before starting at Harrow school in 1881 where he remained until 1886, distinguishing himself as an athlete.

His education at Harrow being successful enough to gain him entrance to Oxford, he began at New College to read law and gained a second-class degree with honours in 1889. Following Lincoln's Inn he was called to the bar in 1890. Despite this recognition he realised that he was not keen to actually begin practising law and so he resolved instead to look after the family's shipping business while specialising himself in Marine Law. This decision saw him take to the seas to destinations such as Vancouver, Island and South AFrica, though it was at the age of twenty-five on one particular journey to Australia, motivated by an (unfulfilled) intention to meet Robert Louis Stevenson on Samoa that he would being to realise fully his literary interests: though he was not considering becoming a writer at this time, his enjoyment of literature was enough to encourage an attempt at meeting a great writer and eventually enabled one of the most significant encounters of his life. He made the journey with his friend Edward Sanderson and, though he missed Stevenson, he met Joseph Conrad, a fellow future author famed for his novels which were often nautically themed. At the time Conrad was the first mate of the sailing-ship Torrens moored in the harbour of Adelaide, Australia; still very much focused on his ship-borne career, he was yet to begin his writing in earnest.

Indeed, though neither knew at the time, both Conrad and Galsworthy were at similar junctures in their lives, their time spent as sea acting as a transitional period during which each found their literary calling. It is perhaps owning to this unknown common ground that they became close friends. During his time on the Torrens Galsworthy recorded several details, offering a frank and valuable characterisation of Conrad while also illuminating his own experiences as a student of Marine Law.

"I supposed to be studying navigation for the Admiralty Bar, would every day work out the position of the ship with the captain. On one side of the saloon table we would sit and check our observations with those of Conrad, who from the other side of the table would look at us a little quizzically."

On his return to England and the cessation of his nautical voyaging, Galsworthy began an affair with the wife of his first cousin, Major Arthur John Galsworthy. Ada Nemesis Pearson Cooper (1864-1956), the daughter of Emanuel Copper, an obstetrician from Norwich, remained married to the Major for ten years and the affair remained secret for its duration. In order to conceal the affair they took considerable pains to avoid suspicion. One such tactic was to stay in a secluded farmhouse called Wingstone in the village on Manaton on Dartmoor, in Devon. In Galsworthy's decision to choose Devon as the location for their clandestine rendezvous we see evidence of Galsworthy's affection for the place of his father's origin. It was only when, in 1905, she divorced the Major that their affair became known following their marriage on 23rd September of that year.

Galsworthy now took to writing sometime after having met Conrad and his career began in earnest when, in 1897, his first work, From the Four Winds, a volume of short stories, was published under the pseudonym John Sinjohn. He succeeded this in 1898 with Jocelyn, his first novel, and then his second in

1900, Villa Rubein. In 1901 he published a second volume of short stories, A Man of Devon, which was the last of his work to be published under pseudonym. The first of his work to be published under his own name was The Island Pharisees in 1904, a novel of social observation, seasoned with flashes of satire and propaganda. His decision to write under his own name is arguably owing to the recent death of his father, either as a mark of respect to his name or because now he was able to publish freely without incurring the possibility of paternal disappointment at his choice of career. It also marked a shift in his professionalism; he had hitherto published with small, independent publishers, but The Island Pharisees was published by Heinemann, a far more established House and one with whom he remained for the duration of his writing career.

He arguably cemented his position and maturity as a writer when, in 1906, he saw the publication of both his first major play, The Silver Box, and the novel The Man of Property. Each was published to considerable critical acclaim, and to achieve both in such a short space of time was impressive. the Silver Box concerns the imbalance in the justice system with regards to criminals of differing class by contrasting the treatment of a poor thief and a rich thief, both of whom stole silver cigarette cases but for very different reasons. The complexity of individual experience when not dealt with in public is highlighted and questioned in a bravely critical manner; despite the clear issues it raises with class and privilege, the final night was attended by the Price and Princess of Wales. The Man of Property was the first novel in the famous The Forsyte Saga, a trilogy of novels with an 'interlude' between each one, written between 1906 and 1921. Dealing with the questions of status, class and materialism, The Man of Property introduces us to the Forsyte family, particularly Soames Forsyte, who is acutely aware of his status as 'new money' and equally keen to assert himself as a wealthy man. Jealous of his wife and desperate to own things in order to confirm his wealth to those observing him, he engineers a plan to keep his wife from her friends which backfires spectacularly when, instead of cutting her off, all Soames achieves is enabling her to have an affair. This drives Soames to terrible actions with terrible consequences, which Galsworthy depicts with confidence.

Very typically Edwardian, the novel focuses on conflict between property and art, and to a certain degree much of its emotional power is drawn from Galsworthy's own life, particularly his affair with Ada. Their rendezvous in the countryside of Devon mirror the manner in which Forsyte seeks to relocate his wife and; though theirs was a much healthier relationship, there are clear similarities. By examining the fragile nature of the class system and those moving within it Galsworthy offered an important perspective on the relationships between material wealth, personal happiness and obsession, and the manner in which these change over time. His contemporaries widely regarded the publication of this novel as marking the end of Victorianism. His friend Conrad praised it as "indubitably a piece of art" and, though the notoriously risqué D.H. Lawrence lamented the novel's timidity in the face of sexuality and sensuality, he considered it potentially "a very great novel, a very great satire".

Though he continued to write both plays and novels, it was his work as a playwright for which he was most celebrated by his contemporaries. Indeed, his next novel, The Country House, seems uncharacteristically unfocused, its satirical view of those belonging to the country set comparatively unremarkable and weakly characterised, while at times the tone of satire becomes one of ironic detachment. In 1909 he published Fraternity, an exploration of of the various connections between urban society and the social classes therein, though its representation of lower-class Londoners is utterly unconvincing and ill-informed. Remaining with the subject of the landed gentry and the society surrounding it, in 1915 he published The Freelands, which does not stray far from conservative discussions of capitalism, the rural economy and their interrelationship.

His drama, however, featured a convincingly muted realism, directed at a relatively small, educated and politically-aware audience. His social agenda is prevalent here too, and is represented in a simple and static manner producing arresting instances of high drama. This talent for creating moments of captivating theatre is complimented by an instinctual sense of balance enabling his narratives to vacillate between their emotional high- and low-points, ultimately reaching conclusive equilibrium. This is particularly evident in one of his most popular plays, Strife, published in 1909 and examining the antagonists in a strike at a Cornish tin mine. In this, and in 1910's Justice, he approaches his subject with sympathy, irony and balance, which establishes a position of narrative authority while garnering the audiences trust that he is representing his characters and their motives justly. Justice condemns the use of solitary confinement in prisons, a reformist agenda which caught the liberality of his contemporary audiences along with the home secretary, Winston Churchill. Despite he was careful to disassociate himself with politics and professed himself apolitical, he and his work were nevertheless aligned with the views of the Liberal establishment. He spent much of the duration of the First World War working in a field hospital in France as an orderly having been passed over for military service.

Despite the popularity and brilliance of his work, it was only in 1920 that he had his first true commercial success with The Skin Game, a melodrama dealing with ethics, property and class. The play was adapted by Alfred Hitchcock in 1931. Galsworthy, meanwhile, had turned down a knighthood in 1918, considering his work not sufficient to be made a knight of the realm. He did, however, accept the Belgian Palmes d'Or in the following year. In 1920 he published the second novel in the Forsyte Saga, In Chancery, in which he resumes many of the themes of the first novel, focusing on the marital disharmony between Soames Forsyte and his wife. Katherine Mansfield considered it "a fascinating, brilliant book" in her review in The Atheneum. Then, in 1921, he was elected as the PEN International Literary Club's first president. The concluding novel to The Forsyte Saga, To Let was published in 1921 with a kind of peace being found between Forsyte and his now-ex wife, though he is left contemplating his losses and his greed. More ironic treatment of class confusions followed in Loyalties, bringing with it more popular success which lasted until 1926 and Escape, the last of his popular plays. Though he enjoyed popular success it was inconsistent and relatively small. His Collected Plays was published in 1929.

Over the course of time the appreciation of his work has gradually shifted from his plays to his novels, and particularly the detail and intricacy of his chronicle of English social difference, tension and pretension in The Forsyte Saga. Its success encouraged Galsworthy to revisit Soames Forsyte in a second trilogy, A Modern Comedy, which follows Soames's obsessive love of his daughter Fleur. In its three volumes, The White Monkey (1924), The Silver Spoon (1936) and Swan Song (1928) he examines the English commercial upper-middle class and its ideologies, its instinct to possess as its only way of distinguishing itself manifested in the poisonous materialism of Soames. Interestingly, this emergent social class which he so vehemently criticises is the very class from which he emerged. He witnessed first-hand its insularity, its chauvinism, its restrictive and oppressive morality, its stubborn imperialism and its materialism, and it is this experience which enables him to write so comfortably about it. Swan Song is widely considered among the best of Galsworthy's writing for the depth of its exploration of society and its heightened emotional subtlety. In 1929 he was appointed to the Order of Merit, despite having turned down a knighthood earlier. He spent his last years writing a third trilogy, End of the Chapter, beginning in 1931 with Maid in Waiting, Flowering Wilderness in 1932 and concluding with Over The River in 1933. These are significantly less coherent works and are indicative of his deteriorating health. Indeed, in 1932 he was awarded the Nobel Prize, though he was too ill to attend the ceremony.

Throughout the course of his career he received honorary degrees from the universities of St Andrews (1922), Manchester (1927), Dublin (1929), Cambridge (1930), Sheffield (1930), Oxford (1931), and Princeton (1931). In 1926 New College, Oxford, elected him as an honourary fellow. In photographs he is portrayed as handsome, fastidiously dressed and dignified. He was unusually compassionate and this saw him involved in several charitable and humane causes throughout the course of his life, including penal reforms, attacks on theatrical censorship and campaigning for animal rights. Though he spent the majority of the final seven years of his life at his home in Bury, West Sussex, it was at his home in Hampstead, London, that he died of a brain tumour on 31st January, 1933, six weeks after having been too ill to attend the ceremony in honour of his receiving the Nobel Prize. According to demands made in his will he was cremated and his ashes scattered over the South Downs from an aeroplane. Also in his will was his wish to leave cottages to several of his astonished tenants. He is memorialised in Highgate 'New' Cemetery and in the cloisters of New College, Oxford, where he was an honourary fellow.

John Galsworthy – A Concise Bibliography

From the Four Winds, 1897 (as John Sinjohn)
Jocelyn, 1898 (as John Sinjohn)
Villa Rubein, 1900 (as John Sinjohn)
A Man of Devon, 1901 (as John Sinjohn)
The Island Pharisees, 1904
The Silver Box, 1906 (his first play)
The Man of Property, 1906 – First book of The Forsyte Saga (1922)
The Country House, 1907
A Commentary, 1908
Fraternity, 1909
A Justification for the Censorship of Plays, 1909
Strife, 1909
Fraternity, 1909
Joy, 1909
Justice, 1910
A Motley, 1910
The Spirit of Punishment, 1910
Horses in Mines, 1910
The Patrician, 1911
The Little Dream, 1911
The Pigeon, 1912
The Eldest Son, 1912
Quality, 1912
Moods, Songs, and Doggerels, 1912
For Love of Beasts, 1912
The Inn of Tranquillity, 1912
The Dark Flower, 1913
The Fugitive, 1913
The Mob, 1914
The Freelands, 1915
The Little Man, 1915
A Bit o' Love, 1915

A Sheaf, 1916
The Apple Tree, 1916
The Foundations, 1917
Beyond, 1917
Five Tales, 1918
Indian Summer of a Forsyte, 1918 – First interlude of The Forsyte Saga
Saint's Progress, 1919
Addresses in America, 1912
In Chancery, 1920 – Second book of The Forsyte Saga
Awakening, 1920 – Second interlude of The Forsyte Saga
The Skin Game, 1920
To Let, 1921 – Third book of The Forsyte Saga
A Family Man, 1922
The Little Man, 1922
Loyalties, 1922
Windows, 1922
Captures, 1923
Abracadabra, 1924
The Forest, 1924
Old English, 1924
The White Monkey, 1924 – First book of A Modern Comedy
The Show, 1925
Escape, 1926
The Silver Spoon, 1926 – Second book of A Modern Comedy
Verses New and Old, 1926
Castles in Spain, 1927
A Silent Wooing, 1927 – First Interlude of A Modern Comedy
Passers By, 1927 – Second Interlude of A Modern Comedy
Swan Song, 1928 – Third book of A Modern Comedy
The Manaton Edition, 1923–26 (collection, 30 vols.)
Exiled, 1929
The Roof, 1929
On Forsyte 'Change, 1930
Two Essays on Conrad, 1930
Soames and the Flag, 1930
The Creation of Character in Literature, 1931 (The Romanes Lecture for 1931).
Maid in Waiting, 1931 – First book of End of the Chapter (1934)
Forty Poems, 1932
Flowering Wilderness, 1932 – Second book of End of the Chapter
Autobiographical Letters of Galsworthy: A Correspondence with Frank Harris, 1933
One More River (originally Over the River), 1933 – Third book of End of the Chapter
The Grove Edition, 1927–34 (collection, 27 Vols.)
Collected Poems, 1934
Punch and Go, 1935
The Life and Letters, 1935
The Winter Garden, 1935
Forsytes, Pendyces and Others, 1935
Selected Short Stories, 1935

Glimpses and Reflections, 1937